Buddhism Day by Day:
Wisdom for Modern Life

BUDDHISM
DAY BY DAY

WISDOM FOR MODERN LIFE

DAISAKU IKEDA

MIDDLEWAY
PRESS

Published by Middleway Press
A division of the SGI-USA
606 Wilshire Blvd., Santa Monica, CA 90401
© 2006 Soka Gakkai

ISBN 978-0-9723267-5-9

Design by Gopa and Ted2, Inc.

10 9 8 7 6 5 4 3 2

Library of Congress Cataloging-in-Publication Data

Ikeda, Daisaku.
  Buddhism day by day : wisdom for modern life /
Daisaku Ikeda.
    p. cm.
  ISBN-13: 978-0-9723267-5-9 (pbk. : alk. paper)
  1. Buddhist devotional calendars.   2. Meditations
—Soka Gakkai.   I. Title.
BQ8499.I384B823 2006
294.3'4432—dc22
                                    2006028530

INTRODUCTION

EVERY DAY, we face new challenges, fresh opportunities for growth. It is in the realm of life's ups and downs, the tempestuous struggles, that Buddhism's value is most keenly demonstrated.

Buddhism is sometimes characterized as a religion of mysticism, practiced in remote temples far from the worries of everyday life. This is a misconception. From the very beginning, the sole purpose of Buddhism has been to lead people to a state of indestructible happiness and wisdom, wherever they are.

Buddhism is a philosophy of life—an engaged and courageous way of being—in which compassion and respect for all people's inherent worth lead to tremendous growth and joy.

The Soka Gakkai International follows the teachings of the thirteenth-century Buddhist reformer Nichiren, who taught that chanting Nam-myoho-renge-kyo was the key to unlocking our ultimate potential, our innate Buddhahood. Nam-myoho-renge-kyo comes from the title of the Lotus Sutra. This phrase is a declaration of the wonderful Dharma, or Law, of causality. Chanting Nam-myoho-renge-kyo accesses an inexhaustible source of fortune and wisdom.

Buddhism Day by Day presents the thoughts of Daisaku Ikeda, president of the Soka Gakkai International and one of the world's leading interpreters of Buddhism. For more than fifty years, Mr. Ikeda has dedicated himself to the worldwide spread of Nichiren Buddhism as the basis for peace and personal fulfillment. Through his efforts for peace, culture and education, he's become a spiritual leader for millions, showing by his own example that all people possess the ability to create value and harmony in society, and between themselves and their environment.

In addition to Mr. Ikeda's thoughts are selections from Nichiren and *The Lotus Sutra*. Together, these short passages give a glimpse into Nichiren Buddhism and can help make each day a victory.

—*The Editors*

About nam-myoho-renge-kyo

CHANTING NAM-MYOHO-RENGE-KYO is essentially a declaration of the enlightened nature in all life, and a vow to manifest it in oneself and others. It is not praise to an external deity but rather the means to manifest Buddhahood, the highest state of life present within all people.

Buddhahood is a state of fearless wisdom and happiness, free of delusion. Buddhahood is also deep compassion; understanding the connection between all life, a Buddha faces the sufferings of all beings and derives joy from teaching others how to awaken to the wondrous potential within.

The Lotus Sutra teaches that in every one of us there exists the potential for terrible suffering and delusion, the potential for Buddhahood and all points in between.

The Lotus Sutra is regarded by Nichiren Buddhists as the most profound teaching of Buddhism. Nichiren declared that the full title, (in Sanskrit, *Saddharma-pundarika-sutra*, translated as *Myoho-renge-kyo*) contains the essence of the sutra itself.

Though Nam-myoho-renge-kyo is meant to be understood as a whole, it can also be viewed word by word. Each syllable contains multiple meanings, but the most basic translation is as follows:

▶ *myo* (*sad*): mystic or wonderful. This represents the wondrous nature of enlightenment.

▶ *ho* (*dharma*): Law, or phenomena. Often *myo* and *ho* are combined as *myoho*, or Mystic Law, meaning the essential truth of Buddhism.

▶ *renge* (*pundarika*): Lotus blossom. This represents the universality of cause and effect. Additionally, a lotus blooms in muddy water, and so a lotus is symbolic of the inherent Buddhahood in all life, no matter how troubled or deluded that life may be.

▶ *kyo* (sutra): Nichiren defined *kyo* as the voice of all living beings, and the eternal truth of Buddhism. As one Buddhist commentary notes, "The voice does the work of the Buddha, and is called *kyo*."

To these characters, Nichiren added *nam*, derived from the Sanskrit word *namas*, meaning devotion or dedication. *Nam* is, in one sense, an action, in other words, to actively devote oneself to the Mystic Law of cause and effect. Thus, in one reading, Nam-myoho-renge-kyo means "devotion to the Lotus Sutra of the wonderful law" and in another reading means, "Devotion to the mystic law of cause and effect through sound."

Through chanting, Nichiren Buddhists awaken their enlightened potential, and from this state, examine the various challenges and benefits in their lives and generate the wisdom to proceed with joy, no matter how great the struggle before them.

—*The Editors*

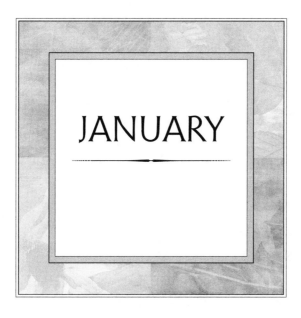

JANUARY

JANUARY 1

IF THE MINDS of living beings are impure, their land is also impure, but if their minds are pure, so is their land. There are not two lands, pure or impure in themselves. The difference lies solely in the good or evil of our minds. It is the same with a Buddha and an ordinary being. While deluded, one is called an ordinary being, but when enlightened, one is called a Buddha. This is similar to a tarnished mirror that will shine like a jewel when polished.

—*Nichiren*

IN NICHIREN BUDDHISM, attaining enlightenment is not about embarking on some inconceivably long journey to become a resplendent, godlike Buddha; it is about accomplishing a transformation in the depths of one's being. In other words, it is not a matter of practicing in order to scale the highest summit of enlightenment at some point in the distant future. Rather, it is a constant, moment-to-moment, inner struggle between revealing our innate Dharma nature or allowing ourselves to be ruled by our fundamental darkness and delusion.

THERE simply are no Buddhas who spend all their time sitting in meditation. Buddhas are Buddhas precisely because they continually ponder and take action to help others resolve their worries.

THE ESSENTIAL teaching of Buddhism is that the life of the Buddha resides in every plant and tree, even in the smallest dust mote. It's a philosophy founded on a profound reverence for life.

ONE OF the epithets of a Buddha is "Hero of the World." A Buddha is a valiant and noble champion who has conquered the sufferings of life in the real world. Nichiren writes: "Buddhism is like the body, and society like the shadow. When the body bends, so does the shadow." People cannot live apart from society. But to be constantly at the mercy of society's ups and downs is a miserable existence. It is crucial for us to be strong and wise. The "body" Nichiren refers to is, on the personal level, our faith.

YOU MUST never think that any of the eighty thousand sacred teachings of Shakyamuni Buddha's lifetime or any of the Buddhas and bodhisattvas of the ten directions and three existences are outside yourself. Your practice of the Buddhist teachings will not relieve you of the sufferings of birth and death in the least unless you perceive the true nature of your life. If you seek enlightenment outside yourself, then your performing even ten thousand practices and ten thousand good deeds will be in vain. It is like the case of a poor man who spends night and day counting his neighbor's wealth but gains not even half a coin.

—Nichiren

HAND IN HAND with (and inseparable from) our personal awakening, the aim of Buddhist practice is to establish a truly peaceful society based on the empowerment of all individuals, a true state of equality and justice grounded in respect for the Buddha nature inherent in everyone.

WISDOM, in the Lotus Sutra, does not simply mean being smart; it is far more profound. Essentially, it is to have an excellent "heart." Wisdom signifies humanity and force of character borne of strength, breadth and profundity of spirit. Nichiren says, "The wise may be called human." He also explains that one who perseveres in following a correct way of life, unswayed by praise and censure, is truly wise.

THE PEACE we seek cannot be brought about through a struggle for dominance in military or economic power. It can be won only through peaceful means. Peace built on the unhappiness and sacrifice of others is a meaningless sham. What's needed is to create a world in which people of all races and nations can enjoy peace and happiness.

THE TWENTIETH CENTURY was a century of war and peace, a century of politics and economics. The twenty-first century holds the promise, however, to be a century of humanity and culture, a century of science and religion. Advance on this wonderful new path of humanism with pride and confidence, as gallant philosophers of action.

ONE TRAGEDY of our times is the willingness of real-
ists, in spite of impending crises, to criticize and
obstruct people who expend their energy toward finding solutions. Their judgments, however, are superficial
and conventional, and their attitude distances them from
the essential quality of reality—change. Often the wis-
est realists cannot escape this trap. The challenge, then,
is to create a new kind of reality that offers hope for
changing the world.

STRENGTH IS HAPPINESS. Strength is itself victory. In weakness and cowardice there is no happiness. When you wage a struggle, you might win or you might lose. But regardless of the short-term outcome, the very fact of your continuing to struggle is proof of your victory as a human being. A strong spirit, strong faith and strong prayer—developing these is victory and the world of Buddhahood.

BUDDHAS respect people's individuality and desire that they may freely manifest their unique qualities. They are neither partial nor adverse toward people on account of their individual proclivities. Buddhas love, rejoice at and try to bring out each person's uniqueness; this is their compassion and their wisdom.

ALWAYS SPEAK the truth boldly, saying what needs to be said no matter whom you're addressing. When it comes to championing a just cause, you must never be cowardly, never fawn, never try to curry favor.

D R. MARTIN LUTHER KING JR., a tireless crusader for human rights, said: "Life's most persistent and urgent question is, 'What are you doing for others?'" Do not say you will do it "someday"; *now* is the time. Do not say "someone" will do it; *you* are the one. Now is the time for youth to take full responsibility and courageously pave the way for the people's triumph.

THE SANSKRIT word *buddha* means "One who is awakened [to the truth]." While the term was widely employed by various schools of the time, it eventually came to be used exclusively in reference to Shakyamuni. At the same time, the word *buddha* implies "to bloom." A person who causes flowers of lofty character to brilliantly bloom and who bears the fruits of good fortune and benefit in abundance is a Buddha. Such a person manifests the benefit of the Law and shines with character overflowing with blessings.

WHEN YOU DEVOTE yourself to achieving your goal, you will not be bothered by shallow criticism. Nothing important can be accomplished if you allow yourself to be swayed by some trifling matter, always looking over your shoulder and wondering what others are saying or thinking. The key to achievement is to move forward along your chosen path with firm determination.

BUDDHISM is practiced to make one's prayers and dreams come true and to achieve the greatest possible happiness. The purpose of Nichiren Buddhism is to enable one to realize victory. The fact that prayers are answered proves the correctness of this teaching.

THE YEARS PASS. The times change. All that survives and transcends this inevitable process, that shines brighter with each new era, is the record of a great human spirit that has endured the unendurable and remained true to the very end to its deepest convictions.

A COMPLETE LACK of exertion or stress may seem desirable, but in fact it results in boredom and stagnation. It is essential that we keep making continuous efforts amid challenging circumstances, pushing forward with dynamic creativity and breaking through all obstacles. That is the way to develop new strength and achieve fresh growth, whether it be in the case of an individual or an organization.

NICHIREN states: "If there are a hundred or a thousand people who uphold this sutra, without a single exception all one hundred or one thousand of them will become Buddhas." All people can attain Buddhahood. Everyone, without exception, can win in his or her own unique way and achieve supreme happiness. That is the greatness of the Mystic Law.

THERE IS a saying that the earth upon which we fall is the same ground which enables us to push ourselves up again. There's another which maintains that barley grows better after it has been trampled on. Human relationships are sometimes painful, but there is no such pain from which we cannot recover. It is up to us to decide to live a life free from self-doubt and despair in spite of our failures. Indeed, it is during our most humbling moments that we should show greatest poise and grace. Then the dignity of our lives will truly shine.

MAHATMA GANDHI SAID, "Good travels at a snail's pace." The peace movement cannot accomplish things radically and all at once. Often, it can only advance by gradual and protracted means. Gradualism does not, however, imply negative compromise or merely passing time. It means truly reforming our times by sowing seeds of peace in individual minds through sincere dialogue and, in this way, cultivating consensus.

BUDDHISM TEACHES equality and absolute respect for the dignity of life. Educating people to be citizens of the world begins with cultivating respect, compassion and empathy for others. I am certain that friendship and limitless trust in people can empower us to overcome socially disruptive discrimination and hatred. Open-minded exchanges on the popular level will be increasingly important in the years to come. When people engage in mind-to-mind dialogue, they are grateful to see ethnic and cultural differences not as obstacles but as expressions of society—enriching diversity that engenders respect and a desire for further exploration.

YOU CANNOT JUDGE the quality of another's friendship by superficial appearances, especially when things are going smoothly. It is only when we have experienced the worst, most crushing of times—when we have plumbed the depths of life—that we can experience the joys of genuine friendship. Only a man of principle, a woman of resolve—a person who stays true to their chosen path—can be a trusted and true friend, and have real friends in turn.

A COWARD cannot become a Buddha. We cannot attain Buddhahood unless we possess the heart of a lion. The harsher the situation, the bolder the stand we must take. This is the essence of the Soka Gakkai spirit.

EVERYONE has a right to flower, to reveal his or her full potential as a human being, to fulfill his or her mission in this world. You have this right, and so does everyone else. This is the meaning of human rights. To scorn, violate and abuse people's human rights destroys the natural order of things. Prizing human rights and respecting others are among our most important tasks.

WHY ARE human beings born? This question has posed a great challenge. Josei Toda lucidly set forward his conclusion. Namely, that this world is a place for people to, as the Lotus Sutra states, "enjoy themselves at ease." We were born here in order to thoroughly savor the joys of life. Faith in Nichiren Buddhism enables one to bring forth the great life force needed to lead such an existence.

I T MAY SEEM perfectly all right to put ourselves and our own wishes first, to simply follow the dictates of our emotions and cravings, but the truth is that there is nothing more unreliable than our own mind. Life doesn't always go like clockwork and things will not necessarily turn out as we hope or plan. Consequently, Nichiren frequently stressed, "You should become the master of your mind, not let your mind master you." We mustn't allow ourselves to be ruled by a self-centered mind. Rather, we have to discipline our mind and gain mastery over it.

JANUARY
30

JUST AS A DIAMOND can only be polished by another diamond, it is only through intense human interaction engaging the entire personality that people can forge themselves, raising themselves up to ever-greater heights.

A HIGHER RELIGION does not negate rationality. No religion that suppresses human reason can earn the trust of humankind. Buddhism, the "religion of wisdom," is an extremely rational religion. In fact, it is so rational that many Westerners even question whether it can be classified as a religion, since it does not teach the existence of a supreme being in the image of humankind.

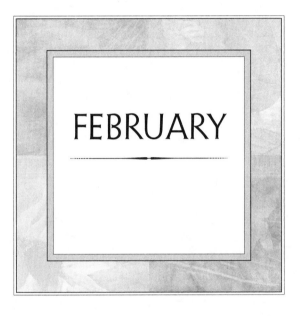

FEBRUARY

WHILE CONTROLLING your mind, which is at once both extremely subtle and solemnly profound, you should strive to elevate your faith with freshness and vigor. When you do so, both your life and your surroundings will open wide before you and every action you take will become a source of benefit. Understanding the subtle workings of one's mind is the key to faith and attaining Buddhahood in this lifetime.

FIRST OF ALL, as to the question of where exactly hell and the Buddha exist, one sutra states that hell exists underground, and another sutra says that the Buddha is in the west. Closer examination, however, reveals that both exist in our five-foot body. This must be true because hell is in the heart of a person who inwardly despises his father and disregards his mother. It is like the lotus seed, which contains both blossom and fruit. In the same way, the Buddha dwells within our hearts.

—*Nichiren*

BECAUSE we live in the human realm, we of course experience problems and suffering. Life is filled with contradictions. But if we refuse to be defeated by them and persist in our faith, we are certain to advance along the path towards happiness and victory. This is the essential power of Buddhism.

YOU MUSTN'T allow yourselves to grow old before your time. Please live with a youthful spirit. That is what Buddhism teaches us to do, and it is how life ought to be lived. If you make a commitment to work for the sake of others, you will be rejuvenated. If you devote your life to helping others, you'll stay young. The power of Nam-myoho-renge-kyo guarantees that.

LIFE FOR EVERYONE is a struggle against the sufferings of birth, old age, sickness and death. Happiness is not the absence of problems or worries; it is to be undefeated no matter what problems or worries we may face. And this happiness is not solely focused on oneself. Truly happy are those who can help others become happy.

THE BUDDHIST VIEW is that to die a good death, one must have led a good life. The knowledge that death represents the return of the individual life to the great universal life prior to another phenomenal manifestation is a source of splendid strength, rich with compassion and wisdom. As he or she strives for self-perfection by doing good for others, the Buddhist is constantly aware that death is a fulfilling and enriching part of life. For people who believe this, death is not defeat, but a wonderful stimulus to live more vigorously and more meaningfully.

IN HIS WRITINGS, regarding Buddhist practice, Nichiren repeatedly emphasized the importance of the heart. While teaching that faith and courage are the powers and functions of the heart that enable us to open the world of Buddhahood in our lives, he also cautioned against the heart's negative functions, such as disbelief and cowardice, which close us off to our potential for Buddhahood.

FEBRUARY

8

JOSEI TODA often compared death to sleep. When we have been awake for a long time, we tire and go to sleep. And when we wake up after a sound sleep, our vitality is restored. After we have been alive for a long time, we grow weary and die. And then we set out on a new life with a fresh spirit. Death is a period of "recharging" for our next existence.

YOU MUST never slacken in your efforts to build new lives for yourselves. Creativeness means pushing open the heavy door to life. This is not an easy struggle. Indeed, it may be the hardest task in the world. For opening the door to your own life is more difficult than opening the doors to the mysteries of the universe.

NICHIREN explains that to know oneself is to know all things in the universe. When you change, your environment changes, too. When your inner resolve changes, everything is transformed. This principle is summed up by Johann Wolfgang von Goethe's maxim, "Nothing's outside that's not within."

THERE WAS A WORD that second Soka Gakkai president Josei Toda often stressed with the fervent wish to impart its importance to his successors. That word was *courage*. He once gave this clear-cut guidance: "The essence of Buddhism is compassion. We, too, need to have compassion but, being ordinary mortals, the reality is that it is quite difficult for us. Courage substitutes for compassion. I am speaking of the courage to save others from suffering. To practice Buddhism with courage translates into compassion."

YOU MAY HAVE fundamental questions about yourself and your identity: Who am I? What should I do with my life? It is quite natural to feel unsure about the best way to proceed. If you haven't yet decided on your future course, I feel the best thing is just to concentrate your energies on what you need to do right now, and gradually your full potential will emerge.

HENRY DAVID THOREAU, a renowned American Renaissance thinker, wrote in his journal: "Nothing must be postponed. Take time by the forelock. Now or never! You must live in the present, launch yourself on every wave, find your eternity in each moment." We shouldn't put anything off but seize the moment, living with all our being in the present. If we do that, he says, each moment will become eternity.

A SHALLOW PERSON will have only shallow relationships. Real love is not one person clinging to another; it can only be fostered between two strong people secure in their individuality. Antoine de Saint-Exupéry, author of *The Little Prince* wrote in a work called *Wind, Sand and Stars*, "Love is not two people gazing at each other, but two people looking ahead together in the same direction."

ENDLESS STRIVING is the only way to realize peace. Negligence resulting from over-confidence and satisfaction invites peril. Peace, once achieved, does not last forever by itself. It requires vigilance throughout all the activities of daily life.

IN THE COURSE of Buddhist practice, various things arise on account of the negative causes and tendencies in our own lives. There may be times when we think, *What did I do to deserve this?* But we should not be swayed every time such phenomena arise; for it is already certain that we will become happy in the end. We should regard as training everything that happens to us in our practice to reach the destination of happiness.

TRUE INDIVIDUALITY never comes to full flower without hard work. Therefore, you're making a big mistake if you think that who you are right now represents all you are capable of being.

LIFE CONTAINS the capacity, like flames that reach toward heaven, to transform suffering and pain into the energy needed for value creation, into light that illuminates darkness. Like the wind traversing vast spaces unhindered, life has the power to uproot and overturn all obstacles and difficulties. Like clear flowing water, it can wash away all stains and impurities. And finally, life, like the great earth that sustains vegetation, impartially protects all people with its compassionate, nurturing force.

CHANG-AN WRITES, "If one befriends another person but lacks the mercy to correct him, one is in fact his enemy." The consequences of a grave offense are extremely difficult to erase. The most important thing is to continually strengthen our wish to benefit others.

—*Nichiren*

WHEN WE PLANT the seeds of self-doubt, only noxious weeds sprout. When we limit ourselves with low expectations, the growth of the tree of happiness immediately ceases. The power of growth, of improvement, the power to overcome all stagnation and break through every obstacle and transform a barren wasteland into a verdant field—that unstoppable power of hope resides right there in your own heart. It will well up from the rich earth of your innermost being when you face the future without doubt or fear: "I can do more. I can grow. I can become a bigger and better human being"—life and faith are a never-ending struggle to grow.

THERE IS no way of life more desolate or more pitiful than one of ignorance of the fundamental joy that issues from the struggle to generate and regenerate one's own life from within. To be human is much more than the mere biological facts of standing erect and exercising reason and intelligence. The full and genuine meaning of our humanity is found in tapping the creative fonts of life itself.

REAL OPTIMISM should not be confused with a carefree outlook on life, one in which we forfeit responsibility for our lives. The person undefeated by misfortune, poverty, insult and vilification, the person who can bounce back from every adversity and say, "What? That was nothing!" The person who marches on toward hope through sheer force of will—that person is a true optimist.

THE ONLY WAY for human beings to change is for them to conquer their inner darkness and rediscover the eternal dignity within their own lives. Cultivating the noble spirit with which all people are endowed will directly lead to a change in the destiny of humankind.

ACCORDING TO Buddhism, health is not a condition in which we merely escape negative influences. It is a highly positive, active state in which we hold ourselves responsible for such influences, in which we face and try to solve various problems—not just our own but others' problems, too. The word *disease* implies a lack of ease, which conversely implies that health is a state of comfort. In the Buddhist sense, however, being "at ease" does not mean freedom from difficulties; it means having the strength to meet and overcome any problem.

WHEN YOU HOLD FAST to your beliefs and live true to yourself, your true value as a human being shines through. Buddhism teaches the concept of "realizing your inherent potential." In other words manifesting your true entity, your innate self, revealing it and bringing it to shine, illuminating all around you. It refers to your most refined individuality and uniqueness.

N O DISCRIMINATION exists in Nichiren Buddhism. Nichiren teaches that the Buddha and all people are absolutely equal. Chanting Nam-myoho-renge-kyo with faith in this point is a matter of the utmost importance. Doing so is to embrace the Lotus Sutra. It is also an act of succeeding to the heritage of Buddhism. In this light, we can say that the gist of the teaching of the Lotus Sutra is that all people are equal.

WE EACH MOVE forward secure on our own earth, not the earth of others. Happiness is something we must create for ourselves. No one else can give it to us.

MAKE GOALS. Whether big or small, work toward realizing them. You must be serious about and dedicated to your goals—you'll get nowhere if you just treat them like jokes. An earnest, dedicated spirit shines like a diamond and moves people's hearts. That is because a brilliant flame burns within.

If we are sincere, people will understand our intentions, and our positive qualities will shine forth. It is pointless to be caught up in outward appearances.

The German poet Johann Wolfgang von Goethe writes: "How may one get to know oneself? Never by contemplation, only, indeed, by action. Seek to do your duty, and you will know at once how it is with you."

WHEN PARENTS exert themselves in the way of faith, they can lead their children to happiness without fail. Likewise, the attainment of Buddhahood of the child guarantees the attainment of Buddhahood of the parents. One lighthouse illuminates the way for many ships to steer a course safely through uncertain waters. In the same way, people with strong and committed faith shine as beacons of hope for their families.

MARCH

WORDS can be either the root of discord or a force for unity. They can be the origin of deception or the key to learning. They can be the instruments of plotting and intrigue or weapons for truth and wisdom. That is why it is so crucial to speak out ever more vigorously for what is right.

MARCH

2

THE IMPORTANT thing is not whether we are optimistic or pessimistic but rather that, while keeping a careful eye on reality, we are neither overwhelmed by it nor content with the status quo. We must keep the lamps of our ideals alight while being ready to pioneer uncharted paths. Faith in life and in the human spirit is the necessary foundation for this approach.

IT ALL COMES DOWN to you. I hope you won't rely on others or wait for them to do something. Try to develop such a strong sense of responsibility that you can stand up to the fiercest storms, confidently proclaiming, "I'll do it. Just watch me!" Please confront reality, look it squarely in the face, and with guts, wisdom and strength, challenge everything that lies ahead of you.

LIFE IS an everlasting struggle with ourselves. It is a tug of war between moving forward and regressing, between happiness and unhappiness. Outstanding individuals didn't become great overnight. They disciplined themselves to overcome their weaknesses, to conquer their lack of caring and motivation until they became true victors in life. One reason Buddhists chant Nam-myoho-renge-kyo each day is to develop strong will and discipline and, along with those, the ability to tackle any problem seriously and with the determination to overcome it.

OUR INDIVIDUAL lives are each infinite treasure houses. Our lives are clusters of blessings. Lasting happiness never comes from the outside. Everything of value emanates from within our own being. Faith in Buddhism means establishing one's true self. It is the recognition that the infinite horizon of the cosmos exists right here within the self. One's life opens out toward the cosmos and is enfolded in it; at the same time, one's life encompasses the entire cosmos.

WHEN WE CHANT Nam-myoho-renge-kyo, the good and evil capacities of our lives begin to function as the exalted form of fundamental existence. Lives that are full of the pain of hell, lives that are in the state of hunger, lives warped by the state of anger—such lives too begin to move in the direction of creating their own personal happiness and value. Lives being pulled toward misfortune and unhappiness are redirected and pulled in the opposite direction, toward good, when they make the Mystic Law their base.

WHEN WE REVERE Myoho-renge-kyo inherent in our own life as the object of devotion, the Buddha nature within us is summoned forth and manifested by our chanting of Nam-myoho-renge-kyo. This is what is meant by "Buddha." To illustrate, when a caged bird sings, birds who are flying in the sky are thereby summoned and gather around, and when the birds flying in the sky gather around, the bird in the cage strives to get out. When with our mouths we chant the Mystic Law, our Buddha nature, being summoned, will invariably emerge.

—Nichiren

N O GREAT ACHIEVEMENT is accomplished overnight or without difficulty. Should benefit be obtained easily without making any efforts in Buddhist practice, we'd probably just as easily abandon our faith and end up miserable as a consequence. Because it isn't easy to get into a highly ranked school, students study with all their might, gaining an abundance of knowledge and ability. Faith follows basically the same formula: Practice is essential to attaining Buddhahood.

SOME PEOPLE are overly critical of themselves and become listless and unassertive as a result. Rather than engaging in pointless self-flagellation, young people would do best just being what young people are: bold, audacious and gutsy—throwing themselves entirely into whatever the task at hand.

THERE IS a great difference between simply living a long life and living a full and rewarding life. What's really important is how much rich texture and color we can add to our lives during our stay here on earth—however long that stay may be. Quality is the true value, not quantity.

THE INDIAN PHILOSOPHER Swami Vivekananda declared: "It is religion, maker of men, that we need. It is education, maker of men that we need." Fostering people, building character—this is absolutely fundamental for creating a bright future. Toward this end, both the profound spirituality of religion and the intellectual illumination of education are essential.

THE HUMAN BEING is not a frail wretch at the mercy of fate. Shakyamuni insisted that to change oneself now is to change the future on a vast scale. The Western impression that Buddhism is all about meditation is alien to the spirit of Shakyamuni. The goal of Nichiren Buddhism is neither escape from reality nor passive acceptance. It is to live strongly, proactively, in such a way as to refine one's own life and reform society through a constant exchange between the outside world and the individual's inner world.

IN THE FACE of rejection, you must learn to be courageous. It is important to believe in yourself. Be like the
sun, which shines on serenely even though not all the
heavenly bodies reflect back its light and even though
some of its brilliance seems to radiate only into empty
space. While those who reject your friendship may
sometimes fade out of your life, the more you shine your
light, the more brilliant your life will become.

DEPENDING ON their outlook, people's old age will dramatically differ, especially in terms of the richness and fulfillment they will experience. Everything is up to our attitude, how we approach life. Do we look at old age as a descending path to oblivion? Or is it a period in which we can attain our goals and bring our lives to a rewarding, satisfying completion?

BUDDHISM comes down to practice. This means making a personal determination and steadfastly taking action to accomplish it, no matter what obstacles may arise. If we aren't striving to open a way forward, what we are doing cannot be called Buddhist practice. We will only enter the path to Buddhahood by making tireless effort based on the same determination as the Buddha.

·

THERE IS no other course for us but to entrust everything to the youth. This holds true for families, businesses and countries. Youth are vitally important to the world and the human race. The key to eternal development lies in fostering, encouraging and training youth who will lead the way to a new era.

MARCH

17

BUDDHISM TEACHES that life at each moment embraces all phenomena. This is the doctrine of a life-moment possessing three thousand realms, which is the Lotus Sutra's ultimate teaching and Buddhism's essence. Because of the profound way our lives interact with people around us, it is vital that we reach out to others, that we be engaged with our environment and with our local community. A self-absorbed practice or theory without action is definitely not Buddhism.

HAPPINESS doesn't exist on the far side of distant mountains. It is within you, yourself. Not you, however, sitting in idle passivity. It is to be found in the vibrant dynamism of your own life as you struggle to challenge and overcome one obstacle after another, as you clamber up a perilous ridge in pursuit of that which lies beyond.

THERE ARE MANY elements involved in a prayer being answered, but the important thing is to keep praying until it is. By continuing to pray, you can reflect on yourself with unflinching honesty and begin to move your life in a positive direction on the path of earnest, steady effort. Even if your prayer doesn't produce concrete results immediately, your continual prayer will at some time manifest itself in a form greater than you had ever hoped.

BUDDHISM aims to make people free in the most profound sense; its purpose is not to restrict or constrain. Buddhist prayer is a right, not an obligation. Because Buddhism entails practice, tenacious efforts are required, but these are all for your own sake. If you want to have great benefits or to develop a profound state of life, you should exert yourself accordingly.

THE FUNCTION of fire is to burn and give light. The function of water is to wash away filth. The winds blow away dust and breathe life into plants, animals, and human beings. The earth produces the grasses and trees, and heaven provides nourishing moisture. The five characters of Myoho-renge-kyo are also like that. They are the cluster of blessings brought by the Bodhisattvas of the Earth, disciples of the Buddha in his true identity.

—Nichiren

LIFE IS FULL of unexpected suffering. Even so, as Eleanor Roosevelt said: "If you can live through that [a difficult situation] you can live through anything. You gain strength, courage and confidence by every experience in which you really stop to look fear in the face. You are able to say to yourself, 'I lived through this horror. I can take the next thing that comes along.'" That's exactly right. Struggling against great difficulty enables us to develop ourselves tremendously. We can call forth and manifest those abilities lying dormant within us. Difficulty can be a source of dynamic growth and positive progress.

I AM THE FATHER of living beings and I should rescue them from their sufferings and give them the joy of the measureless and boundless Buddha wisdom so that they may find their enjoyment in that.

—*The Lotus Sutra*

THE STRUGGLE we go through to have our prayers answered makes us stronger. If we were to immediately get everything we prayed for, we would become spoiled and decadent. We would lead indolent lives, devoid of any hard work or struggle. As a result, we would become shallow human beings. What, then, would be the point of faith?

THE SIGNIFICANCE of Buddhism lies both in the discovery of the Buddha nature in all beings and in the establishment of a practical method for bringing it out, so that human beings can derive maximum meaning from their lives. This reformation of the inner human world—what we in the Soka Gakkai call "human revolution"—is especially relevant to modern civilization, which has long been trapped in a sort of spiritual quicksand. We can escape the quicksand by calling forth the supreme human potential available to each of us.

WHEN EXPERIENCING failures and disappointments, frustrations or illness, people tend to lose confidence and let fear overtake them. At such times, however, we need to make a conscious effort to move forward with strength and courage. When you say to yourself, "Next time I'll succeed!" or "I'm going to get better and make it through this!" you have already won.

BY CHANGING our inner state of mind, we can change any suffering or hardship into a source of joy, regarding it as a means for forging and developing our lives. To turn even sorrow into a source of creativity—this is the way of life of a Buddhist.

A BUDDHA is definitely not an absolute being living a static existence. A Buddha shares the sufferings of others and, sensing the condition of the time, earnestly ponders how to transform that condition. A Buddha vows to struggle in order to lead the people and the age to enlightenment. The strength of this vow causes the Buddha's enlightenment to mature into rich wisdom.

NICHIREN SPOKE of earthly desires being used as fuel for the flame of wisdom. Buddhism teaches the converting of personal ambitions and desires, even base ones, into good traits like wisdom through altruistic living. A Buddhist doctrine that earthly desires *are* enlightenment indicates that greed, anger (violence) and egocentricism can be transformed into altruistic traits like compassion, trust and nonviolence. The underlying delusions that drive our desires—including the desire for the development of science and civilizations—can be essentially transformed in a way that changes selfishness into altruism, violence into nonviolence and suspicion into trust.

IT IS IMPORTANT to develop your character to be as powerful as a mighty river. Continue to advance bravely in the face of every challenge, paying no heed to the obstacles in your way. Become a great river of bottomless compassion and wisdom, overflowing with boundless invincibility and passion.

READING is dialogue with oneself; it is self-reflection, which cultivates profound humanity. Reading is therefore essential to our development. It expands and enriches the personality like a seed that germinates after a long time and sends forth many blossom-laden branches.

People who can say of a book "this changed my life" truly understand the meaning of happiness. Reading that sparks inner revolution is desperately needed to escape drowning in the rapidly advancing information society. Reading is more than intellectual ornamentation; it is a battle for the establishment of the self, a ceaseless challenge that keeps us young and vigorous.

APRIL

A T ALL TIMES I think to myself:
How can I cause living beings
to gain entry into the unsurpassed way
and quickly acquire the body of a Buddha?

—The Lotus Sutra

PROMPTNESS is crucial in leading a victorious life. How we start each morning determines that day's victory or defeat. It's important that we resolve to win in the morning and begin our work with an energetic, refreshed spirit. We mustn't forget that this is the secret to continual success. We live in a tumultuous age, and in such times, swift action is the key to success.

A LIFE LIVED without purpose or value, the kind in which one doesn't know the reason why one was born, is joyless and lackluster. To just live, eat and die without any real sense of purpose surely represents a life pervaded by the life-state of animals. On the other hand, to do, create or contribute something that benefits others, society and ourselves and to dedicate ourselves as long as we live up to that challenge—that is a life of true satisfaction, a life of value. It is a humanistic and lofty way to live.

THE FLOWER of the Law blooms within the human being. It shines through our character. The Lotus Sutra is wholly a teaching for human beings. The purpose of religion is to help each person become happy. But even a teaching whose original intent was to promote human happiness may start to restrict people. Even the Lotus Sutra could be used incorrectly to justify discrimination. What is necessary to prevent the danger of such distortion from occurring? It is the disciple's inheritance of the resolute spirit and faith of the mentor to lead people to happiness.

EVEN PLACES that have been shrouded in darkness for billions of years can be illuminated. Even a stone from the bottom of a river can be used to produce fire. Our present sufferings, no matter how dark, have certainly not continued for billions of years—nor will they linger forever. The sun will definitely rise. In fact, its ascent has already begun.

PURE and committed practice of Nichiren Buddhism entirely changes the meaning of hardships in our lives. We no longer view challenges and trials as negatives to be avoided but as things which, when overcome, bring us closer to our attainment of Buddhahood.

THE BUDDHIST teaching of the inseparability of evil and good means that everything can be made one or the other in an instant, according to what we harbor in our hearts. Everything begins with the self. A change in one's outlook or intention triggers a change in the self and radiates outward to effect society-wide revolutions. This idea is what we in the SGI refer to as "human revolution."

N ICHIREN WRITES, "If you light a lantern for another, it will also brighten your own way." Please be confident that the higher your flame of altruistic action burns, the more its light will suffuse your life with happiness. Those who possess an altruistic spirit are the happiest people of all.

I LLUSION about the true nature of existence is literally illusion about the nature of one's own life. This is the fundamental source of all illusions. If we are ignorant about the nature of our own existence, then we will be ignorant about the nature of other people's lives, too. On the other hand, when our lives are free of illusion, we can perceive the treasure tower that shines resplendent in all people, in all beings.

MANY TODAY regard any kind of belief—and religious faith, in particular—as somehow in opposition to reason or at the very least as a sort of paralysis of the faculty of reason. There are, indeed, fanatical religions in which faith opposes reason. But it is an erroneous leap of logic to assume on this basis, and without any evidence, that all religions are so. That itself is irrational and can be characterized as a kind of blind faith in its own right.

WORTHY PERSONS deserve to be called so because they are not carried away by the eight winds: prosperity, decline, disgrace, honor, praise, censure, suffering, and pleasure. They are neither elated by prosperity nor grieved by decline.

—*Nichiren*

APRIL

12

I'T'S IMPORTANT to remember that your prayers always reflect your state of life. In that respect, prayer is a solemn means to raise your life-condition. And to get exactly the results that you're praying for, it is crucial to make determined, single-minded efforts toward that goal. That is the true path of manifesting faith in daily life. Those of you who proceed along this path day after day, year after year, will without fail develop—just like saplings into mighty trees—becoming people of out-standing strength and character.

A GREAT WORK of art is one that truly moves and inspires you. You yourself must be moved. Don't look at art with others' eyes. Don't listen to music with others' ears. You must react to art with your own feelings, your own heart and mind. If you allow yourself to be swayed by the opinions of others—"It must be good because everyone else likes it," "It must be bad, because no one else likes it"—your feelings, your sensibility, which should be the very core of the artistic experience, will wither and die. To enjoy art to the fullest, you must abandon all preconceived notions, leaving a blank slate. Then confront the work directly, with your entire being. If you are deeply moved, then that work is, for you, a great work of art.

THE TENDENCY of human beings is to try and escape challenges and seek an easy and peaceful environment. But happiness cannot be found somewhere else—it is found within us. A genuine way of life consists of transforming where we are right now into a supreme paradise.

L IFE AND DEATH are one, and the entity of our existence is eternal, persisting throughout past, present
and future. The setting sun, radiant with joy, gives proof
of its undiminished power and at the same time offers a
promise of a bright tomorrow. Bringing our lives to a
wonderful, satisfying close guarantees us the path to
happiness throughout eternity.

UNLESS ACTED ON, even the ideal of reverence for life can end up being a mere slogan without the power to transform reality. It must, therefore, be established as a genuine philosophy in our hearts and in the hearts of others. We must put this philosophy into practice through concrete actions for peace, working one step at a time toward its realization.

THE GOAL is not to eliminate desires; it is what one desires that is important. Earthly desires are enlightenment. The desire for supreme enlightenment, the search for enlightenment, is enlightenment. Satisfaction with one's accomplishments might seem like humility, but to underestimate life's potential is actually great arrogance.

WE LIVE in the midst of a flood of soulless information. And, the more we rely on one-way communication, like radio or TV, or static and unmoving words in print, the more I feel the need to stress the value of the sound of the human voice: The simple but precious interaction of voice and voice, person and person; the exchange of life with life.

GRASS AND TREES cannot grow without soil. The "soil" that fosters our growth includes our parents, teachers, seniors, or homeland, alma mater, community or company. In any case, everyone has some place where they grew up or someone who nurtured them. Human beings grow as a result of nurturing "soil" in which they express their ability and make the flowers of their lives blossom, just as the spirit of the rice plant returns to the soil and the stalk sprouts to flower and bear grain once again. We should repay our debts of gratitude to this soil in which we developed. This cycle of repaying gratitude will envelop one's whole existence. Your true humanity will never blossom if you seek only to develop yourself.

JUST AS FLOWERS open up and bear fruit, just as the moon appears and invariably grows full, just as a lamp becomes brighter when oil is added, and just as plants and trees flourish with rain, so will human beings never fail to prosper when they make good causes.

—*Nichiren*

THERE ARE many people, many lives, on this planet, too numerous, in fact, to count. From this great multitude, we wondrously find ourselves together with those in our families— as parents and children, as brothers and sisters, as husbands and wives. If we do not live joyfully and cheerfully in the company of those with whom we share this profound bond, what is life for? Should the atmosphere at home be somber, you yourself can be the "sun." By being a shining presence, you can cast the light of hope on your father, mother and whole family.

DO NOT COMPARE yourselves to others. Be true to who you are and continue to learn with all your might. Even if you are ridiculed, even if you suffer disappointments and setbacks, continue to advance and do not be defeated.

WHEN WE are aware that each moment of each day, each gesture and step we take, is truly mystical and full of wonder, we will live our lives with greater thought and care. We will also have greater respect and appreciation for the lives of others.

THE BUDDHAS, the World-Honored Ones, wish to open the door of Buddha wisdom to all living beings, to allow them to attain purity. That is why they appear in the world. They wish to show the Buddha wisdom to living beings, and therefore they appear in the world. They wish to cause living beings to awaken to the Buddha wisdom, and therefore they appear in the world. They wish to induce living beings to enter the path of Buddha wisdom, and therefore they appear in the world.

—*The Lotus Sutra*

IF YOU THINK about it, although we may not be destined to die five minutes from now, we are all, without
exception, going to die at some point. We can count on
it 100 percent. There is nothing surer than this. Victor
Hugo says, "We are all under sentence of death, but with
a sort of indefinite reprieve." Ideally, we should live
every minute of our lives valuably, as if it were the last
moment of our lives. Those who live aimlessly are left
with a sense of emptiness at the end of their lives, but
those who live all-out, striving right to the end, will die
peacefully. Leonardo da Vinci says, "As a well-spent day
brings happy sleep, so life well used brings happy
death." One aware that death could come at any time
will live each day to the fullest.

AS GLOBALIZATION proceeds, we enter an age in which everybody's actions strongly influence everybody else. When we realize this, we can then alter our mindset and strive to build a global society of mutual coexistence and mutual prosperity. This will be done by going beyond devotion to the interests of the nation-state and devoting ourselves to the interests of all humanity. As Dr. Martin Luther King Jr. said, injustice anywhere is a threat to justice everywhere. The key to the solution is the imagination to care for others. It is the empathizing heart or what Buddhists refer to when they talk about mercy.

WE ALL LONG for things of beauty—beauty of nature, of appearance, of life, a beautiful family and so on. But these cannot be gained if we are withdrawn and isolated, just looking at ourselves. We must create better relationships with other people and interact with our community and society with an open heart. We must be kind to nature. It is only through this process that we really grow and cultivate our own beauty.

APRIL
28

WHEN DELUDED, one is called an ordinary being, but when enlightened, one is called a Buddha. This is similar to a tarnished mirror that will shine like a jewel when polished. A mind now clouded by the illusions of the innate darkness of life is like a tarnished mirror, but when polished, it is sure to become like a clear mirror, reflecting the essential nature of phenomena and the true aspect of reality. Arouse deep faith, and diligently polish your mirror day and night. How should you polish it? Only by chanting Nam-myoho-renge-kyo.

—*Nichiren*

OUR EFFORTS for the sake of dialogue, in order to be worthy of the term *dialogue*, must be carried through to the end. To refuse peaceful exchange and choose force is to compromise and give in to human weakness; it is to admit the defeat of the human spirit. Socrates encourages his youthful disciples to train and strengthen themselves spiritually, to maintain hope and self-control, to advance courageously, choosing virtue over material wealth, truth over fame.

NICHIREN wrote that wrath can be either good or bad. Self-centered anger generates evil, but wrath at social injustice becomes the driving force for reform. Strong language that censures and combats a great evil often awakens adverse reactions from society, but this must not intimidate those who believe they are right. A lion is a lion because he roars.

MAY

NICHIREN states, "Mugwort that grows in the midst of hemp, or a snake inside a tube [will as a matter of course become straight], and those who associate with people of good character will consequently become upright in heart, deed, and word." If we apply this passage to various influences upon children, we may say that the environment surrounding children, particularly the behaviors of adults, has a great impact on children. Parents must set good examples before nagging them to do this or that. Parents must strive to become a good, upright influence for children like hemp for mugwort. It is also important for parents to bring their children closer to "people of good character" outside their own families so that children may advance in a more positive direction.

MAY

2

GREAT PEOPLE never forget what others have done for them. In fact, having a sense of appreciation makes a person worthy of respect.

THE SGI is a gathering of ordinary people. We struggle to ensure that the people are not despised and exploited by the powerful. To help all people become strong and wise, we are developing a network of peace and culture and putting great effort into education. By nature, the people are strong, wise, cheerful and warm. Religious faith has the power to draw out those qualities. The purpose of faith is not to turn people into sheep; it is to make them wise. Wisdom isn't knowledge that causes suffering for others; it is enlightened insight for improving one's own life as well as the lives of others.

WHAT BUDDHISM terms *good friends* are sincere, honest people without a trace of deceit who guide others toward the correct path, toward good. It also refers to people who lend their assistance or support to us so that we can practice Buddhism with full assurance.

If you become close to a person who makes you feel "that person is always glowing and animated" or "When I'm with that person I feel strong and secure," then your faith will naturally deepen, and you will develop bountiful wisdom. In carrying out this Buddhist practice, encountering good friends is the key to obtaining Buddhahood.

WHEN YOU encounter a wall, you should tell your-self, "Since there is a wall here, a wide, open expanse must lie on the other side." Rather than becoming discouraged, know that encountering a wall is proof of the progress that you have made so far.

CHANTING Nam-myoho-renge-kyo is the foundation of Nichiren Buddhism. When we chant sonorously, the sun rises in our hearts. We are filled with power. Compassion wells forth. Our lives are lit with joy. Our wisdom shines. All Buddhas and protective forces throughout the universe go to work on our behalf. Life becomes exhilarating.

MAY

7

SUFFER what there is to suffer, enjoy what there is to enjoy. Regard both suffering and joy as facts of life, and continue chanting Nam-myoho-renge-kyo, no matter what happens. How could this be anything other than the boundless joy of the Law? Strengthen your power of faith more than ever.

—*Nichiren*

WILDFLOWERS are neither vain nor haughty, neither jealous nor servile. Living in accord with their unique mission, characterizing the Buddhist principle of the equality of cherry, peach, plum and damson blossoms, they neither envy other flowers nor belittle themselves. They take pride in their individuality, knowing that each is a flower with a bloom like no other. Even the prettiest and most delicate wildflowers are by no means weak. They may seem fragile, but they are strong, unperturbed by rain or wind.

A TURKISH PROVERB says, "Iron shines when used, but rusts when not." The capacities of people working hard and striving with all their might never get rusty; they are constantly being polished and forged.

CHILDREN remember all their lives mothers who are always optimistic and generous toward society and the community and who live creatively. That kind of behavior provides the finest possible nourishment for learning how to build a happy home life. It is important for married couples, while giving full rein to their individual characteristics, to cooperate for the happiness of the children, the family and society.

THE SANCTITY of life is known to everyone. At the same time, there is universal confusion about the essential meaning of life's sanctity. If the sanctity of life can become a solid touchstone of wisdom for all people, then humankind's destiny to experience war and misery repeatedly can be greatly transformed. It is toward this end that we Nichiren Buddhists are struggling.

HUMAN SOCIETY, as viewed with the "eyes of Buddhism," takes on a completely different meaning from that discerned by "secular eyes." No longer are the powerful above and ordinary people below. Status does not make people great, and authority does not make them noble. Instead, it is people wholeheartedly dedicated to a lofty ideal who shine the brightest.

WE SHOULD give first priority to the development of an independent spirit as a human being before considering one's role as a man, woman, child or parent. In other words, for a person to become a man, woman, child or parent in the true sense of the word, one has to first of all develop his or her autonomous identity as a human being.

WHAT CAN the individual accomplish in the face of the huge institutions that run our world? This feeling of powerlessness fuels a vicious cycle that only worsens the situation and increases people's sense of futility. At the opposite extreme of this sense of powerlessness lie the Lotus Sutra's philosophy of three thousand realms in a single moment of life and the application of this teaching to our daily lives. This principle teaches us that the inner determination of an individual can transform everything; it gives ultimate expression to the infinite potential and dignity inherent in each human life.

WHEN WATER is clear, the moon is reflected. When the wind blows, the trees shake. Our minds are like the water. Faith that is weak is like muddy water, while faith that is brave is like clear water. Understand that the trees are like principles, and the wind that shakes them is like the recitation of the sutra.

—*Nichiren*

IN A RELATIONSHIP, it is demeaning to constantly seek your partner's approval. Such relationships are bereft of real caring, depth or even love. For those of you who find yourselves in relationships where you are not treated the way your heart says you should be, I hope you will have the courage and dignity to decide that you are better off risking the scorn of your partner than enduring unhappiness with him or her.

WISDOM is rooted in the souls of human beings. The way to acquire it is to follow the simple advice of Socrates: "Know thyself." This is the starting point for the establishment of a sense of human dignity, preventing the degradation of human beings into anonymous, interchangeable cogs in a machine. The essence of true knowledge is self-knowledge.

NICHIREN BUDDHISM is concerned with a very practical problem—how people should live their lives—and never for an instant allows its attention to be diverted from that problem. And because this is its purpose, it demands as a first step that one conduct a thorough and fearless examination into the true nature of human life.

MAY
19

NICHIREN was utterly convinced we could change even the most dire and painful reality, including the danger of war, and, indeed, that it was imperative we do so. This conviction underlies his unwavering determination to create a peaceful society by widely disseminating the teachings of Buddhism.

MAY

20

THE LOTUS SUTRA has the drama of fighting for justice against evil. It has a warmth that comforts the weary. It has a vibrant, pulsing courage that drives away fear. It has a chorus of joy at attaining absolute freedom throughout past, present and future. It has the soaring flight of liberty. It has brilliant light, flowers, greenery, music, paintings, vivid stories. It offers unsurpassed lessons on psychology, the workings of the human heart; lessons on life; lessons on happiness; and lessons on peace. It maps out the basic rules for good health. It awakens us to the universal truth that a change in one's heart can transform everything.

THE BEST WAY to attain Buddhahood is to encounter
a good friend. How far can our own wisdom take
us? If we have even enough wisdom to distinguish hot
from cold, we should seek out a good friend. But encountering a good friend is the hardest possible thing to
do. For this reason, the Buddha likened it to the rarity of
a one-eyed turtle finding a floating log with a hollow in
it the right size to hold him, or to the difficulty of trying to lower a thread from the Brahma heaven and pass
it through the eye of a needle on the earth.

—*Nichiren*

ONLY WITHIN the open space created by dialogue, whether conducted with our neighbors, with history, with nature or the cosmos, can human wholeness be sustained. We are not born human in any but a biological sense; we can only learn to know ourselves and others and thus be trained in the ways of being human. We do this by immersion in the ocean of language and dialogue fed by the springs of cultural tradition.

I BELIEVE that whether we can live a truly satisfying life to the end depends to a considerable extent on how we view death. Sadly, many older people are anxious and fearful about death. But, as a Buddhist, I find it helpful to compare the cycles of life and death to the daily rhythms of waking and sleeping. Just as we look forward to the rest sleep brings after the efforts and exertions of the day, death can be seen as a welcome period of rest and re-energizing in preparation for a new round of active life. And just as we enjoy the best sleep after a day in which we have done our very best, a calm and easy death can only follow a life lived to the fullest without any regrets.

MAY

24

THE ULTIMATE and most glorious of human relationships is the relationship of spiritual successors. Even
animals have relationships of parent and child. There
are animals that share partnerships similar to marriage,
and even those that enjoy friendships. However, the
relationship of mentor and disciple, of spiritual successors, exists only among human beings.

THE INDIAN POET Rabindranath Tagore compares the function of evil to the banks of a river. The riverbanks are obstructions, but they are necessary for keeping the river on track and flowing steadily forward. Without banks, the river would overflow, causing destruction instead of creating value.

MAY
26

THERE IS a saying that "Speech is silver, silence is golden." But when you are engaged in a struggle, the opposite is true. Then, speaking out is golden and silence is defeat.

SIMILAR to the unifying and integrating self that Carl Jung perceived in the depths of the ego, the term *greater self* in Buddhism expresses the openness and expansiveness of character by which we can embrace all people's sufferings as our own. The greater self always seeks to alleviate pain and to augment the happiness of others here amid the realities of everyday life. Furthermore, the dynamic, vital awakening of the greater self enables each individual to experience both life and death with equal delight.

THE BELIEF taught in the Lotus Sutra provides no easy answers, no escape route from the difficulties of human life. In fact, it rejects such easy answers; instead it implores us to take up the two tools for exploring life, belief and understanding, and use them to continually challenge and work to perfect ourselves. And it also provides us the energy to do just that.

SHAKYAMUNI proclaims, "People who are vigilant do not die; people who are negligent are as if dead." This is definitely true. Unremitting diligence in our Buddhist practice—brave and vigorous exertion—infuses our lives with the great life force of the eternal Buddha. In contrast, people who try to get by in life through cunning and deception enact a living death.

ALL CHILDREN are gems, full of precious potential. There is hope in every child since life itself is full of hope. Should the hopes of children be stifled or broken, that would be our responsibility as adults. It pains my heart to see what goes on in today's society. I do not want to see the eyes of children darkened with fear and clouded with tears of sorrow. Society must be absolutely transformed. Children are mirrors that reflect adult society. When adults are ailing and their vision clouded, children will also suffer. Let us wipe away the tears of sorrow from the face of each child! We must protect children and give them courage, strength and vitality. It is parents who nurture children, the hope of humanity. How noble parents are! What a great mission and responsibility they fulfill.

THE POETIC SPIRIT encourages people in all ranks and places to return to their naked humanity. Neither sentimental nor fantastic, it embraces and affirms the whole world and all its inhabitants; it imparts the will to remain optimistic and unbending in the face of all hardships.

As a believer in innate human goodness, I am certain that the concentrated power of good can overcome the greatest forces of evil. The poetic spirit helps us control the greed-dominated self. It helps us handle the actual while keeping our eyes turned toward the ideal.

JUNE

WHAT IS TRUE JOY in life? This is a difficult question—and one that has occupied a great many thinkers and philosophers. Joy can quickly give way to suffering. Joy is short and suffering long. Also what passes for joy in society is superficial. It cannot compare with the joy deriving from the Mystic Law. The key then lies in cultivating a state of mind where we can declare without reservation that life itself is a joy. This is the purpose of our Buddhist practice.

JUNE
2

UNLESS we can perceive our fellow human beings and feel their sufferings as our own, we will never be free of conflict and war. In other words, a transformation within our own lives is important.

WHEN WE PLANT the seed of happiness that is faith and carefully tend its growth, it will produce fruit without fail. We have to bear in mind, however, that we cannot plant a seed today and expect it to bear fruit tomorrow. That's not reasonable and Buddhism is reason. If we persevere, bearing in mind the principle faith equals daily life in accord with reason, then our prayers will definitely be answered. This is Nichiren's promise to us. And his words are true beyond any doubt.

IT'S SO IMPORTANT to keep the promises made to friends. This is the true meaning of friendship. To become people who can do so, however, we must first learn to keep our resolutions—the promises we have made to ourselves.

EVERYTHING starts with you. You must forge yourself through your own efforts. I urge each of you to create something, start something and make a success of something. That is the essence of human existence, the challenge of youth. Herein lies a wonderful way of life always aiming for the future.

JUNE

6

I HAVE PROFOUND reverence for you, I would never dare treat you with disparagement or arrogance. Why? Because you are all practicing the bodhisattva way and are certain to attain Buddhahood.

—The Lotus Sutra

NAM-MYOHO-RENGE-KYO enables us to make any hardship or setback the source of our new advancement and our treasure for the future. Therefore, you don't have to be afraid of making a mistake or encountering an obstacle. In short, as long as you are devoted to staying in the correct orbit of faith, you won't ever cease to advance toward your victory, even if you may go through some twists and turns in life.

JUNE

8

EVERY CHILD is precious. The Lotus Sutra tells the parable of the three kinds of medicinal herbs and two kinds of trees. There are many different kinds of plants; their shape, size and nature come in myriad varieties. Some plants grow fast while others take time to mature. In this parable, however, the heavens rain upon all the plants equally, nurturing their growth. And the plants blossom and bear fruits according to their own unique character. This parable symbolizes the Buddha's vast compassion to nurture all living beings despite their differences. All children are different; each possesses his or her wonderful unique quality. We must pour upon all children our great love and compassion so that each child can blossom, true to his or her unique quality.

I N ANY FIELD of endeavor, making a vow is the foundation for achieving something great. If for whatever reason a person gives up halfway or backslides, his or her commitment hasn't been based on a vow. Halfhearted desire doesn't amount to a vow.

"ALL RIGHT, let's get to work again!"—this is the spirit of people of genuine substance. Those who avoid hard work or neglect the things they have to do, who just while away their time, eating, sleeping, playing, watching television—such individuals will never experience true happiness, satisfaction or joy.

LIFE IS about scaling one mountain, then facing the next one, followed by the one after that. Those who persevere and finally succeed in conquering the highest mountain are victors in life. On the other hand, those who avoid such challenges and take the easy route, descending into the valleys, will end in defeat.

JUNE

12

THERE MAY BE TIMES when life seems gloomy and dull. When we feel stuck in some situation or other, when we are negative toward everything, when we feel lost and bewildered, not sure which way to turn—at such times we must transform our passive mind-set and determine, "I will proceed along this path," "I will pursue my mission today." When we do so a genuine springtime arrives in our hearts, and flowers start to blossom.

NO ONE can escape death. Precisely because of this, when people resolve to live at each instant with all their might, to make the present moment shine by living true to themselves and leading truly humane existences, they can summon forth immense strength. At the same time, they can manifest a considerate spirit toward others. Herein lies the Middle Way. Buddhism is the philosophy that teaches this essential way of life.

WHEREVER we are, it is necessary to begin with the revitalization of individual human beings. That will lead to the reformation of society and the world through human revolution. That is the teaching of the Lotus Sutra. And actions directed toward that end, I would like to stress, represent the wisdom of the Lotus Sutra.

THE JOY of heaven is ephemeral like a mirage or a dream. A life spent in pursuit of a mirage is itself a mirage. The purpose of Buddhist practice is to establish an eternally indestructible state of happiness, not a fleeting happiness that perishes like a flower but an internal palace of happiness that will last throughout all time.

THE WRITER Johann Wolfgang von Goethe was an unflagging optimist. How was he able to maintain such optimism? Because he was always active. He did not allow his life to stagnate. He writes, "It is better to do the smallest thing in the world than to hold half an hour to be too small a thing." Spending thirty minutes a day assiduously challenging some undertaking can completely change our lives.

WHEN WE INTERACT with others with true sincerity, the other person will more often than not come to respect and value our own character. And this is all the more so when our actions are based on prayer.

Conversely, holding others in contempt only leads to being held in contempt oneself: one whose life is tainted by feelings of hate toward others will come to be reviled by others.

Let us open the path to mutual respect and harmonious coexistence so as to bring an end to this vicious circle that has long been part of human destiny.

WHAT DECIDES our real merit as human beings?
Ultimately, it comes down to the philosophy we
uphold and the actions we take based on our convictions.

IF YOU always have a shallow perspective and pay attention only to trivial things, you are sure to get bogged down in all kinds of petty worries and concerns, and not be able to move forward. Even relatively minor hurdles or problems will seem insurmountable. But if you look at life from a broad viewpoint, you naturally spot the way to solve any problem you may confront. This is true when we consider our own personal problems as well as those of society and even the future of the entire world.

BUDDHISM elucidates the dignity of human life on the most fundamental level. Buddhism is not merely a philosophy that observes truth from an objective point of view or in light of reason. It is oriented toward practice and the study of human beings that shows the correct way to live. Buddhism aims to prove the true dignity of human life through the individual's life and his or her actions to help others do the same. In other words, Buddhism is a practice to revere human life, one's own as well as others'.

CERTAINLY there will be times when you wish you had more spending money, more time to sleep and more time for fun and recreation. You may feel restricted now, but you should consider your current situation as the perfect set of circumstances for your growth. Within the restrictions that define your present existence, the only thing to do is to discipline yourself and head in the direction of growth and self-improvement.

JUNE

22

THE BUDDHA keenly understands various sufferings as though his own children were experiencing them. Sorrow and empathy well from his life. A Buddha is a person of compassion. Josei Toda said: "Compassion is not a Buddhist austerity. It is something that should be expressed unconsciously and naturally in one's actions, and in the workings of one's heart. The Buddha knows no path of living apart from that of living with compassion."

IF A PERSON is hungry, we should give them bread. When there is no bread, we can at least give words that nourish. To a person who looks ill or is physically frail, we can turn the conversation to some subject that will lift their spirits and fill them with the hope and determination to get better. Let us give something to each person we meet: joy, courage, hope, assurance, philosophy, wisdom, a vision for the future. Let us always give something.

FLINT HAS the potential to produce fire, and gems have intrinsic value. We ordinary people can see neither our own eyelashes, which are so close, nor the heavens in the distance. Likewise, we do not see that the Buddha exists in our own hearts.

—*Nichiren*

THE FIRST THING is to pray. From the moment we begin to pray, things start moving. The darker the night, the closer the dawn. From the moment we chant Nam-myoho-renge-kyo with a deep and powerful resolve, the sun begins to rise in our hearts. Hope— prayer is the sun of hope. To chant each time we face a problem, overcoming it and elevating our life-condition as a result—this is the path of "changing earthly desires into enlightenment," taught in Nichiren Buddhism.

THIS LIFETIME will never come again; it is precious and irreplaceable. To live without regret, we must have a concrete purpose, continually setting goals and challenges for ourselves. And we need to keep moving toward those specific targets steadily and tenaciously, one step at a time.

WHEN individuals practice a teaching as intended, the expected result becomes manifest in their lives as well as in their environment. Religion not only deals with spirituality but also has a significant impact—positive or negative—upon people's daily lives and their society. The nature and extent of a particular religion's impact becomes the standard for evaluating its validity.

IF **YOU** are unwilling to make efforts to heal yourself, it will be very difficult to cure your illness. One day of life is more valuable than all the treasures of the major world system, so first you must muster sincere faith.

—*Nichiren*

ORIGINALLY, every person's life is a brilliantly shining mirror. Differences arise depending on whether one polishes this mirror: A polished mirror is the Buddha's life, whereas a tarnished mirror is that of a common mortal. Chanting Nam-myoho-renge-kyo is what polishes our lives.

IN ONE of his writings, renowned microbiologist René Dubos, stated. "History teaches that man without effort is sure to deteriorate; man cannot progress without effort, and man cannot be happy without effort." This is indisputable. You may be experiencing various hardships now, but because you continue to make efforts in the midst of those challenges, no matter how painful they are, you will definitely become happy. Effort and happiness are indivisible.

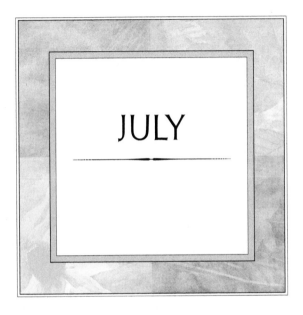

JULY

IF WE CHERISH the spirit to repay our debt of gratitude in the depths of our hearts, then our good fortune will increase by leaps and bounds. No matter how much action people might seem to be taking outwardly, if they lack the spirit to repay their debt of gratitude, their arrogance will destroy their good fortune.

IF WE ATTAIN the state of Buddhahood in this lifetime, that state will forever pervade our lives. Throughout the cycle of birth and death, in each new lifetime, we are endowed with good health, wealth and intelligence, along with a supportive, comfortable environment, and lead lives that overflow with good fortune. Each of us will also possess a unique mission and be born in an appropriate form to fulfill it.

A MENTOR is indispensable if we are to develop into people of outstanding character. Viewed on a deeper level, our relationship with our mentor can have an even greater significance for us than our relationship with our parents. In the mentor-disciple relationship, we can find the very essence for achieving victory in life.

A GREAT inner revolution in just a single individual will help achieve a change in the destiny of an entire society and, further, will cause a change in the destiny of humankind.

JULY

5

HAVING the energy to argue is a sign of good health! When the two people in a relationship share similar conditions, it is only natural that they will lock horns from time to time. On the other hand, if one party begins to outgrow the other, then the two will probably not have serious confrontations, because their states of life are so different.

It would be great if we could live cheerfully, enjoying life to the extent that we regard our partner's nagging as a sign of his or her good health and proof that he or she is still alive and kicking. When we develop a broad state of life, then even our partner's ranting and raving will sound like the sweet song of a bird.

A STRONG opponent helps us develop and forge our own strength and ability. When you encounter some challenge, rejoice and say to yourself, "I have met a rare and worthy adversary!" Greet everything positively, weather all storms with a strong, resilient spirit, and emerge triumphant. That is the Buddhist way of life.

BUDDHISM, which is founded on the law of cause and effect, stresses the concept of karma. This principle explains that life at each moment is subject to the cumulative effects of causes made in the past. What we do, what we say and what we think are all causes. And according to Buddhism, the moment we do something, say something or think something, an effect is registered in the depths of our being. Then, as our lives meet the right circumstances, the effect becomes apparent. Personality traits are strongly connected to our karma. The good news is that, unlike fate, our karma can be changed by causes we make from this moment forward. In fact, the practice of Buddhism is essentially the practice of continually changing our karma.

BUDDHISM concerns itself with winning. When we battle a powerful enemy, either we will triumph or we will be defeated—there is no middle ground. Battling against life's negative functions is an indivisible part of Buddhism. It is by being victorious in this struggle that we become Buddhas. We have to win. Moreover, Buddhism ensures that we can definitely do so.

WHEN OPEN and engaged, we are experiencing the greater self. When closed off, we are putting forth our "lesser self." The lesser self is a deluded condition, while the greater self is synonymous with the Buddha nature. To live for the greater self means to recognize the universal principle behind all things and, thus awakened, rise above the suffering caused by awareness of impermanence. A belief in something eternal is needed to enhance our quality of existence. By believing this lifetime is the be-all and end-all of existence, we will miss out on living a truly profound life. When our viewpoint expands beyond the boundaries of our present existence to include the entire, eternal universe, we can live deeply fulfilling lives.

PEOPLE'S HEARTS are growing more complex, more confused and harder to understand. The same is true for human institutions. The darkness of this complicated and disturbed age may grow even deeper. This is why there is an even greater need for the brilliant inner light of culture, for education that polishes people's wisdom and character. This is the key to winning in life.

THE HEART of the Buddha's lifetime of teachings is the Lotus Sutra, and the heart of the practice of the Lotus Sutra is found in the "Never Disparaging" chapter. What does Bodhisattva Never Disparaging's profound respect for people signify? The purpose of the appearance in this world of Shakyamuni Buddha, the lord of teachings, lies in his behavior as a human being.

—*Nichiren*

N O ONE can better bask in summer's balm than those who have endured winter's bite. Similarly, it is those who have suffered through life's darkest hours who are able to truly savor the bright dawn of happiness. The person who has transformed the worst of fate into the best of fortune is life's champion.

PEOPLE shouldn't hesitate to exert their all, in a way true to themselves. How can you possibly ever know how far or fast you can go if you've never run all-out? To give up even before you've tried is actually arrogance—an affront to the wondrous power of life within you and disrespectful to yourself. It is cowardly.

AN AWARENESS of death enables us to live each day each moment—filled with appreciation for the unique opportunity we have to create something of our time on earth. I believe that in order to enjoy true happiness, we should live each moment as if it were our last. Today will never return. We may speak of the past or of the future, but the only reality we have is that of this present instant. And confronting the reality of death actually enables us to bring unlimited creativity, courage and joy into each instant of our lives.

DAILY LIFE can seem all too drab and unexciting. Living itself can sometimes seem a strain, and few of us realistically expect what joy we feel to last forever. But when we fall in love, life seems filled with drama and excitement. We feel like the leading character in a novel. But, if you get lost in love just because you are bored, and consequently veer from the path you should be following, then love is nothing more than escapism.

WHAT WILL the future be like? No one knows the answer to this question. All we know is that the effects that will appear in the future are contained in the causes made in the present. The important thing, therefore, is that we stand up and take action to achieve great objectives without allowing ourselves to be distracted or discouraged by immediate difficulties.

HUMAN BEINGS inherently possess the strength to overcome any hardship. Religions have traditionally taught the importance of such spiritual strength. This is Buddhism's point of origin. Shakyamuni Buddha taught us to strive to win happiness and peace, not outside but within ourselves.

PEOPLE of conviction, who stand alone, who pursue their chosen path—not only are such people good and trustworthy friends themselves, but they can make genuine friends of others. The bamboo groves of autumn are gorgeous. Each bamboo tree stands independently, growing straight and tall toward the sky. Yet in the ground, out of sight, their roots are interconnected. In the same way, true friendship is not a relationship of dependence, but of independence. It is the enduring bond that connects self-reliant individuals, comrades who share the same commitment, on a spiritual dimension.

IT'S FOOLISH to be obsessed with past failures. And it's just as foolish to be self-satisfied with one's small achievements. The present and the future are what are important, not the past. Those who neglect this spirit of continual striving will start to veer off in a ruinous direction.

ALTHOUGH I and my disciples may encounter various difficulties, if we do not harbor doubts in our hearts, we will as a matter of course attain Buddhahood. Do not have doubts simply because heaven does not lend you protection. Do not be discouraged because you do not enjoy an easy and secure existence in this life. This is what I have taught my disciples morning and evening, and yet they begin to harbor doubts and abandon their faith.

—Nichiren

WE CAN lose ourselves in romantic attachment, but the truth is, the euphoria is unlikely to last for long. Indeed, the likelihood of undergoing suffering and sadness only grows over time. As long as we remain unable to redress our own weaknesses, we will be miserable no matter where or to whom we may take flight. We can never become truly happy unless we ourselves undergo a personal transformation.

JOSEI TODA always urged us to live our lives with courage and never be cowards. He said: "Those who can't do anything but live cowardly lives are like beasts. They are ignoble and unhappy. Those who live out their lives courageously, on the other hand, lead the noblest and most sublime existences; they are happy."

I'VE SUGGESTED that the twenty-first be named the Century of Women. Women have the wisdom and strength to lead society in the direction of good, of hope and of peace. In expanding his own nonviolence movement, Mahatma Gandhi greatly relied on women. He said it is women who can teach pacific learning to a world that, while engaged in hostilities, nonetheless thirsts for the sweet dew of peace.

THE ARGENTINE educator Almafuerte wrote: "To the weak, difficulty is a closed door. To the strong, however, it is a door waiting to be opened." Difficulties impede the progress of those who are weak. For the strong, however, they are an opportunity to open wide the doors to a bright future. Everything is determined by our attitude, by our resolve.

MANY PEOPLE talk about peace, but few really do anything about it. Very few are willing to fight the battle to the end. Josei Toda instilled in me the hard and fast rule that, even if we stand alone, we must never give up but must see the struggle through to its conclusion.

The year before he died, he said something I have never forgotten for a minute: "If we don't fight, justice will be defeated. Because justice is on our side, we must not lose, we absolutely must win. That's why we fight. The lion is most lionlike when he roars."

WHAT DOES attaining Buddhahood mean for us? It does not mean that one day we suddenly *turn into* a Buddha or become magically enlightened. In a sense, attaining Buddhahood means that we have securely entered the path, or orbit, of Buddhahood inherent in the cosmos. Rather than a final static destination at which we arrive and remain, achieving enlightenment means firmly establishing the faith needed to keep advancing along the path of absolute happiness limitlessly, without end.

THE BRILLIANCE of true humanity lies in surmounting feelings of envy with the resolute attitude "I'll create an even more wonderful life for myself." If you are jealous of others, you will not advance; you will only become miserable. Please do not be defeated or consumed by such emotions.

THE BUDDHA'S compassion is perfectly equal and impartial. The Buddha views all beings as his own children and strives to elevate them to attain his same enlightened state of life. It's not that there are no differences among people. Rather, it's that the Buddha, while fully recognizing people's differences, does not discriminate among them.

COMPASSION is the very soul of Buddhism. To pray for others, making their problems and anguish our own; to embrace those who are suffering, becoming their greatest ally; to continue giving them our support and encouragement until they become truly happy—it is in such humanistic actions that Nichiren Buddhism lives and breathes.

RELIGION must teach an "attitude to life." To live a life of true human dignity is certainly difficult. Life is change; it is continuous change. Nothing is constant. The four sufferings of birth, old age, sickness and death are an eternal theme that no one can escape.

Amid harsh reality, people yearn from the depths of their beings to live with dignity and for their lives to have meaning, and they make efforts toward that end. The product of these human yearnings, these prayers, is religion. Religion was born from prayer. What is Nichiren's response to these prayers of human beings? What attitude toward life does he teach? The answer, in short, is the principle of attaining Buddhahood in this lifetime.

WHAT is the purpose of life? It is happiness. But there are two kinds of happiness: relative and absolute. Relative happiness comes in a wide variety of forms. The purpose of Buddhism is to attain Buddhahood. In modern terms, this could be explained as realizing absolute happiness—a state of happiness that can never be destroyed or defeated.

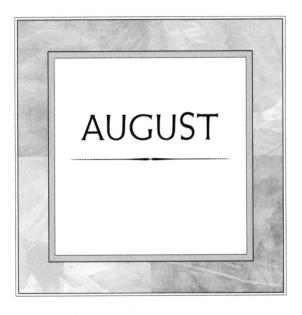

AUGUST

B Y WHOLEHEARTEDLY and directly meeting life's chal-lenges, we bring forth from within ourselves the "three bodies of the Buddha," which are truth, wisdom and compassion. The light of this internal wisdom con-stantly encourages and guides us toward true and cor-rect action.

WHY WAS Shakyamuni Buddha so respected? One of the reasons was the power of his voice. His voice is recorded as "beautiful, sweet like honey, warm and graceful, resounding and clear." He is also described as an individual who "speaks brightly, remarks brightly, narrates gracefully, talks clearly, expresses himself eloquently to make himself understood."

Shakyamuni called to anybody who visited him, "Welcome, welcome." It is expounded that he associated with people with his friendliness, joy and gentleness. He always politely greeted any person he encountered. He never greeted them in an unfriendly manner. It is said that he first opened his mouth to speak to the other person so that he or she would have an easier time to open up to Shakyamuni.

BE RESOLVED to summon forth the great power of faith, and chant Nam-myoho-renge-kyo with the prayer that your faith will be steadfast and correct at the moment of death. Never seek any other way to inherit the ultimate Law of life and death, and manifest it in your life. Only then will you realize that earthly desires are enlightenment, and that the sufferings of birth and death are nirvana. Even embracing the Lotus Sutra would be useless without the heritage of faith.

—*Nichiren*

IN BUDDHIST TERMS, the great universe and the self—the great macrocosm and the microcosm—are one. Since the self and all phenomena are one, all things are interrelated. Termed *dependent origination*, this teaching explains that all things weave a single whole in which individuals live in relation to all others.

In other words, all beings and phenomena exist or occur because of their relationship with other beings and phenomena, and nothing in either the human or the nonhuman world exists in isolation. All things are mutually related to and interdependent with all other things. They all form a great cosmos maintaining the rhythms of life.

BUDDHIST optimism is not the escapist optimism of those who throw up their hands and say, "Somehow or other things will work out." Rather it means clearly recognizing evil as evil and suffering as suffering and resolutely fighting to overcome it. It means believing in one's ability and strength to struggle against any evil or any obstacle. It is to possess a fighting optimism.

PRAYER in Nichiren Buddhism is fundamentally a vow. It is a pledge or commitment to follow a chosen course of action; it is a declaration to challenge a clear objective. As such, how could anything be more wonderful than the vow to realize our personal human revolution and actualize the goal of world peace?

THE PEOPLE we are close to are important. We should treat them as our treasures. When dealing with others, we should always be sincere and polite. Nothing is stronger than sincerity.

I have made many friends around the world and made them all with the same sincerity. A relationship built with sincerity will never be destroyed, but relationships build by means of tactics and scheming always collapse in the end.

DEPENDING on the use to which it is put, religion can be a demonic force. Religion should bring us together, but it is exploited by some to create greater schisms among us. Nothing could be more unfortunate. Religion must always be for the people. People do not exist for the sake of religion. This must be the fundamental guideline of religion in the twenty-first century.

FAITH AND daily life, faith and work—these are not separate things. They are one and the same. To think of them as separate—that faith is faith, and work is work—is theoretical faith. Based on the recognition that work and faith are one and the same, we should put 100 percent of our energy into our jobs and 100 percent into our faith, too. When we resolve to do this, we enter the path of victory in life. Faith means to show irrefutable proof of victory amid the realities of society and in our own daily lives.

THE HEART of one person moves another's. If one's own heart is closed, then the doors of other people's hearts will also shut tight. On the other hand, someone who makes all those around him or her into allies, bathing them in the sunlight of spring, will be treasured by all.

AUGUST

11

ONE who has mastered himself is truly free. Freedom lies in the heart of the sage, servitude in the heart of the fool.

WHEN YOU LOOK at those of superior capacity, do not disparage yourself. The Buddha's true intention was that no one, even those of inferior capacity, be denied enlightenment. Conversely, when you compare yourself with persons of inferior capacity, do not be arrogant and overproud. Even persons of superior capacity may be excluded from enlightenment if they do not devote themselves wholeheartedly.

—Nichiren

BUDDHISM teaches that human life is endowed simultaneously with both good and evil. The human mind is interpreted as partaking of ten different conditions, or states, including, at one end of the scale, hell, which is filled with suffering; hunger, dominated by greed; and animality, characterized by fear of the strong and contempt for the weak. At the other end are the Bodhisattva and Buddha conditions—states of mind in which people strive to help others by eliminating suffering and imparting happiness. Buddhism further teaches that the nature of life is for good and evil to be essentially inseparable.

IN NICHIREN Buddhism, we are encouraged to chant Nam-myoho-renge-kyo for the happiness of those who—for whatever reason—displease, anger or even hurt us. Often this is not easy. But, inevitably, we come to see the better side of most people.

THE WORLD is growing increasingly interrelated and interdependent. We have reached a point where, in order to deal with not only environmental problems but every other issue confronting humankind, leaders with a broad, global perspective are indispensable. Everything hinges on how many capable leaders we can produce who are willing to fight wholeheartedly for the world's future and the happiness of humanity.

AS LONG AS we are human, we are bound to make mistakes. We all fall prey to flawed beliefs and views. What distinguishes a forward-looking person from an intransigent one, a virtuous person from a dishonest one, however, is whether one can candidly admit to one's mistakes and take bold steps to redress them.

THE BUDDHIST teaching of the oneness of life and its environment tells us that humanity and the natural world are one. That is why if we wish to protect the environment, we must transform and purify the three poisons—greed, anger and foolishness—that exist in people's lives. The principle of human revolution focuses on precisely that: inner transformation at the most fundamental level.

PERHAPS the chief purpose of a philosophy or religion is to help us understand the meaning of death and why we are alive. Without understanding where we have come from and where we are going, we cannot establish our own sense of identity to the fullest. Aging and its symptoms can, if nothing else, prompt us to seek rejuvenation. Ultimately, that rejuvenation can be found not in forestalling symptoms but in embracing a larger understanding of our own lives, which Buddhism elucidates.

ULTIMATELY, we are responsible for our own destiny. It may seem to us that our fate is predetermined, whether by our genes or by our environment. What really matters, however, is how we can improve ourselves from this moment forward, how we can change the circumstances that we find ourselves in. This enormous transformative force is what Buddhism is all about. In this struggle lies the source of never-ending youth and vitality.

NATURE is like a mirror. It remains still, but I move. It seems unchanging, yet I am constantly changing. The mirror of nature reflects my inner world, the essence of humanity, and the great, all-embracing expanse of life itself. Only when we are connected to nature, engaged with nature, are we truly alive and vigorous. To really be alive, one must be under the sun, the moon, the shining stars and surrounded by the beautiful greenery and pure waters of the natural world.

IT IS IMPORTANT to remember that your worth as a person is not based on your profession. It is not based on wealth, fame or academic credentials. What counts is how hard you have striven in your chosen path, how much good you have accomplished, how earnestly you have devoted your energies to it. It is your spirit of devotion, your sincerity, that determines your true worth.

THE TIMES when I have most intensely felt and experienced the inner reality of creation have been those times when I have thrown myself wholeheartedly into a task, when I have carried through with that task to the very end. At such times, I experience a dramatically expanded sense of self. I can almost hear the joyous yell of victory issuing from the depths of my being.

RALPH WALDO EMERSON says, "Good-nature is plentiful, but we want justice with a heart of steel, to fight down the proud." If people are merely good-natured, then those who are arrogant and highhanded will have free rein to carry on as they please. Only those who fight with hearts of steel are people of justice.

AUGUST
24

IT HAS BEEN said that aging gracefully is more difficult than dying, but as long as we have a forward-looking, positive attitude, a spirit to take on challenges, we will gain depth in our lives.

ONE OF the fascinating things about human beings is this: Believe for long enough that you are not as smart as others and this will actually lead to intellectual ineptitude. But, confronted with the same doubts, if you choose to believe that your mind is merely dormant for now, lacking in exercise, once you begin to train it, there are no bounds to what you can achieve.

THERE IS no trace of coercion or concern for appearances in Nichiren's behavior. He looked on those who were suffering, those who were bravely fighting alongside him, as if they were himself in the same situations. He prized each and every one of them. He encouraged them and sympathized with them, and we must never forget that the true essence of humanity is to be found in this. When we observe Nichiren's actions, we are deeply struck by the conviction that this is the way a Buddhist must live.

WHEN we create or appreciate art, we set free the spirit trapped within. That is why art arouses such joy. Art—whether skillfully executed or not—is the emotion, the pleasure of expressing life as it is. Those who see art are moved by its passion and strength, its intensity and beauty. That is why it is impossible to separate life from art. Political and economic developments may seem to dominate the news, but culture and education are the forces that actually shape an age, since they transform the human heart.

ANGER is fundamentally an arrogant state of life. People in the state of anger are attached to the illusory assumption that they are better than others and direct their energy toward sustaining and enhancing this image. To ensure that others think of them in similarly glowing terms, they can never reveal their true feelings. Instead, they act obsequiously while a burning desire to surpass all others is their exclusive focus. With their inner feelings and their outward appearance out of accord, they don't speak from the heart. Buddhism teaches that the heart is most important. Of two people making comparable efforts, the results will differ greatly if one person is motivated by a value that transcends the self—good, beauty, the well-being of others—while the other is motivated by ego.

THOUGH one might point at the earth and miss it, though one might bind up the sky, though the tides might cease to ebb and flow and the sun rise in the west, it could never come about that the prayers of the practitioner of the Lotus Sutra would go unanswered.

—Nichiren

BUDDHISM stresses the interconnectedness of all life. It is only the limited capacity of our senses that causes us to place so much stock in the separation between "them" and "us." Because of this interconnectedness, by using violence, you not only injure or destroy the other person but also yourself. Those who use violence and devalue others' lives actually devalue and ruin their own lives.

OVERCOMING the four sufferings of birth, old age, sickness and death is not just a matter of theory. We mustn't move away from the issues of how we can lead healthy, fulfilling and long lives, and how we can die without suffering. Buddhism teaches the wisdom that enables us to do this.

SEPTEMBER

WE MUST establish the correct standard of value upon the foundation of the dignity of life. Leaders of society, including politicians and schoolteachers, should teach children the distinction between good and evil and lead society in the direction of goodness. Today, however, the higher the status that people achieve, the more wrongdoings they tend to commit. Those in high status think only of their selfish interests while exploiting ordinary people. The "me first" attitude prevails. Looking at those adults, children cannot possibly grow upright. Such social trends, in a sense, are destroying our children. Adults must first reflect on their own way of life. Without self-reflection, adults are not qualified to scold children.

ULTIMATELY, happiness rests on how you establish a solid sense of self or being. Happiness does not lie in outward appearances nor in vanity. It is a matter of what you feel inside; it is a deep resonance in your life. To be filled each day with a rewarding sense of exhilaration and purpose, a sense of tasks accomplished and deep fulfillment—people who feel this way are happy. Those who have this sense of satisfaction even if they are extremely busy are much happier than those who have time on their hands but feel empty inside.

VIEWING EVENTS and situations in a positive light is important. The strength, wisdom and cheerfulness that accompany such an attitude lead to happiness. To regard everything in a positive light or with a spirit of goodwill, however, does not mean being foolishly gullible and allowing people to take advantage of your good nature. It means having the wisdom and perception to actually move things in a positive direction by seeing things in their best light, while all the time keeping your eyes firmly focused on reality.

WHAT WAS the secret to Thomas Edison's success? He explained that it was to never give up before he succeeded in what he was trying to do. Not giving up—that's the only way. Once you give up you are defeated. This is equally true in the realm of faith. Quitting is not faith. We have to keep chanting until our prayers are answered. That is the correct way of prayer.

I N *The Record of the Orally Transmitted Teachings*, Nichiren says, "Difficulties will arise, and these are to be looked upon as 'peaceful' practices." You may wonder how encountering difficulties could be viewed as a source of peace. But the truth of the matter is that through struggling against and overcoming difficulties, we can transform our destiny and attain Buddhahood. Confronting adversity, therefore, represents peaceful practice.

THERE IS nothing wrong with being successful in society and enjoying a degree of fame. But ultimately, the lives of those dedicated to the welfare and happiness of others, even if they remain unrecognized, are the ones truly worthy of respect.

HOW PAINFUL and frightening is the prospect of death for human beings! No matter how wealthy or powerful we may be, all is vanity before death. Everything is empty, like a dream or an illusion. But people do not face this fact.

Nichiren Buddhism teaches us that we can transform our karma and attain a supremely peaceful death that is the start of a journey to our next lives.

THE GERMAN author Herman Hesse writes that the more one matures, the younger one grows. Certainly there are many people who as they age become increasingly vigorous and energetic, more broad-minded and tolerant, living with a greater sense of freedom and assurance. It is important to remember that aging and growing old are not necessarily the same thing.

WHAT MATTERS is winning in the end; the wins and losses along the way are of secondary significance. It's final victory in life that counts and that is the reason for our Buddhist practice. No matter how powerful or famous or privileged a person might be, Nichiren says, from a Buddhist point of view it is all nothing more than a dream, an illusory pleasure; true happiness can only be attained by revealing the state of Buddhahood within your own life.

NEITHER the pure land nor hell exists outside oneself; both lie only within one's own heart. Awakened to this, one is called a Buddha; deluded about it, one is called an ordinary person. The Lotus Sutra reveals this truth, and one who embraces the Lotus Sutra will realize that hell is itself the Land of Tranquil Light.

—Nichiren

SEPTEMBER

11

I F WE ARE to survive, a stronghold of peace must be fashioned within the mind of every single man, woman and child on the earth. This stronghold must resolutely hold out against the invasion of any idea to make war.

BUDDHISM teaches that all people are inherently Buddhas. I believe that this Buddhist view of humanity embodies a fundamental principle for world peace. You are a Buddha and I am a Buddha. That's why we must not fight each other. That's why we must respect each other.

EXERTING YOURSELF by chanting Nam-myoho-renge-kyo each day amounts to what might be called a spiritual workout. It purifies and cleanses your life, gets your motors running and puts you on the right course for the day. It gets your body and mind working smoothly and puts you in rhythm, in sync, with the universe.

THE BUDDHA does not look down on living beings from on high. He lifts them up to the same level as himself. He teaches them that they are all equally treasure towers worthy of supreme respect. This is the philosophy of the Lotus Sutra and Nichiren's spirit. It is true humanism.

WHEN ONE is deluded, it is as if one were dreaming. And when one is enlightened, it is as if one had awakened.

—*Nichiren*

ONE THING is certain: That is that the power of belief, the power of thought, will move reality in the direction of what we believe and conceive of it. If you really believe you can do something, you can. That is a fact.

LIFE CAN UNFOLD unlimitedly as long as we have a heart of appreciation and an undefeated mind. Based on the Buddhist perspective of the eternity of life, we volunteered to be born in our current life-condition and chose to encounter the problems we have. If you can take this perspective, you should be able to overcome any difficulty with joy.

YOU HAVE been able to accept, uphold, read, recite and ponder this sutra and to preach it for others. The good fortune you gain thereby is immeasurable and boundless. It cannot be burned by fire or washed away by water. Your benefits are such that a thousand Buddhas speaking all together could never finish describing them. Now you have been able to destroy all devils and thieves, to annihilate the army of birth and death, and all others who bore you enmity or malice have likewise been wiped out.

Good man, a hundred, a thousand Buddhas will employ their transcendental powers to join in guarding and protecting you. Among the heavenly and human beings of all the worlds, there will be no one like you.

—*The Lotus Sutra*

THE HIGHEST offering to the Buddha is not to worship something reminiscent of the Buddha. Rather, it is to inherit the Buddha's spirit. In other words, the highest offering lies in struggling to manifest, as one's own way of life, even a part of the spirit of the Buddha, who upheld the philosophy that everyone is a Buddha and tirelessly strove to save all from suffering.

THERE HAS never been, nor will there ever be, a Buddha who does not encounter hardships. Only by struggling against difficulties can we attain the life-state of Buddhahood. Herein lies the essence of Buddhism.

EFFORTS to reach out and engage others in dialogue with the aim of fostering mutual understanding and bringing people closer together may seem ordinary and unexciting, but they in fact constitute a bold and daring challenge to create a new era of human civilization.

BUDDHISM views illness as an opportunity to attain a higher, nobler state of life. It teaches that, instead of agonizing over a serious disease, or despairing of ever overcoming it, we should use illness as a means to build a strong, compassionate self, which in turn will make it possible for us to be truly victorious.

NOW, if you wish to attain Buddhahood, you have only to lower the banner of your arrogance, cast aside the staff of your anger, and devote yourself exclusively to the one vehicle of the Lotus Sutra. Worldly fame and profit are mere baubles of your present existence, and arrogance and prejudice are ties that will fetter you in a next one.

—Nichiren

WE ARE ALL human beings, whatever our positions. If we open our hearts and speak with sincerity, we can communicate and touch others on the deepest level. World peace starts with trust between one individual and another.

IN THE TRUE reality of life as viewed from the enlightened state of the Buddha—who has broken free of all delusion—all things are equal, transcending distinctions and differences between subject and object, self and others, mind and body, the spiritual and the material. In its true aspect, life is infinitely expansive and eternal, without beginning or end. Life is dynamic; it is wisdom and compassion; it embodies the principle of the indivisibility of life and death; it is a universal law. The cosmos is not so big that life cannot embrace it, nor a particle of matter so small that life cannot be contained within it.

LIVE in a way that is full of life—for yourself, for your loved ones, for your friends. People who do so will find the courage to transform sufferings into hopes. Not only that, but they will be able to light the lamp of hope in the hearts of many others as well.

THE WISE course is to control and make correct use of knowledge. Buddhism is a means for developing wisdom, and it teaches how to overcome the four inherent sufferings or sorrows—birth, aging, illness and death—in order to lead a happy, meaningful life. In addition it teaches how to control desire rather than be controlled by it.

YOUR HOME is where your loved ones live. Your home is the place where you work together with your fellow human beings to build a paradise, a realm of peace and prosperity for all. When we are asked where our home is, we can answer: "My home is the world. Everywhere in the world where my fellow human beings live, all of it, is my home."

A SWORD is useless in the hands of a coward. The mighty sword of the Lotus Sutra must be wielded by one courageous in faith. Then one will be as strong as a demon armed with an iron staff.

—*Nichiren*

KNOWLEDGE gives rise to wisdom. If you like, knowledge is the pump; wisdom is the water that we get from the pump. If we can't obtain water, the pump is useless. At the same time, without knowledge, without the pump, we won't be able to obtain water.

OCTOBER

TIME IS constantly passing, one moment following fast upon the other. That's why it's so important to press forward boldly, without complaining or fretting. The person who looks to the future and keeps moving ahead is eternally youthful. Such a person's heart is filled with flowers and shines brilliantly.

OUR INDIVIDUAL circle of friendship is part of the global circle of friendship; it is one and the same. A drop of rain from the sky, a drop of water from the river, or a drop of water from the ocean are all just that—a drop of water—until they accumulate. The friends we make in our own small circle contribute to the spread of friendship around the world. Making one true friend is a step toward creating world peace.

BUDDHISM teaches that self-awareness arises through our encounters with the eternal. Buddhism urges us to be receptive to the most profound meaning of living, in the eternal process of cosmic evolution, and further urges that we accept, as our mission, compassionate behavior toward all beings.

THE EXPANSIVE world lies not in some distant place; it exists right where you are. That is why you need to win where you are right now. Today's victory is linked to your eternal victory.

NO MATTER what the circumstances, you should never concede defeat. Never conclude that you've reached a dead end, that everything is finished. You possess a glorious future. And precisely because of that, you must persevere and study. Life is eternal. We need to focus on the two existences of the present and the future and not get caught up in the past. We must always have the spirit to begin anew "from this moment," to initiate a new struggle each day.

I F YOU SUMMON your courage to challenge something, you'll never regret it. How sad it would be to spend your life wishing, "If only I had a little more courage." Whatever the outcome, the important thing is to take a step forward on the path that you believe is right. There's no need to worry about what others may think. It's your life, after all. Be true to yourself.

IF YOU REMAIN sincere in your interactions with others, you will one day find yourself surrounded by good friends. And among those people, your friendships will be as strong and unshakable as towering trees. *Don't be impatient.* Work first on developing yourself, and you can rest assured that an infinite number of wonderful encounters await you in the future.

LIFE IS LIKE a sea voyage. We each need to open up our own course in life with the strength of our convictions, unperturbed by the crashing breakers of life's stormy seas. The fiercer the tempest rages, the more we need to rouse our own fighting spirit and man the tiller with all our strength and skill crying, "Bring it on!" Through this type of arduous struggle we can forge the practical wisdom to triumph consistently and, as victorious champions, to create history.

THOSE WHO SAY "I'll do it," who are willing to take on a challenge even if they are alone, are true winners. The determination, the commitment to take action yourself, is the force that leads to victory. As Buddhism teaches in the principle of a life-moment possesses three thousand realms, our mind or attitude can change everything.

SHAKYAMUNI TAUGHT that the shallow is easy to embrace, but the profound is difficult. To discard the shallow and seek the profound is the way of a person of courage.

—*Nichiren.*

OCTOBER
11

I T'S VALUABLE to look for the strengths in others—you gain nothing by criticizing people's imperfections. In fact, it is helpful to take a step back, for even a moment each day, and try to consider the feelings and positive qualities of others of whom you are critical.

TODAY there are people who have faith in the Lotus Sutra. The belief of some is like fire while that of others is like water. When the former listen to the teachings, their passion flares up like fire, but as time goes on, they tend to discard their faith. To have faith like water means to believe continuously without ever regressing.

—*Nichiren*

JOSEI TODA explained the supreme benefit of faith as follows: "Attaining Buddhahood means achieving the state in which we are always reborn overflowing with abundant and powerful life force; we can take action to our heart's content based on a profound sense of mission; we can achieve all our goals; and we possess good fortune that no one can destroy." The purpose of faith is to realize a state of eternal happiness. This existence is as fleeting as a dream. We practice faith to awaken from this dream and firmly establish a state of eternal happiness in the depths of our lives during this lifetime.

OCTOBER

14

LIFE IS best lived by being bold and daring. People tend to grow fearful when they taste failure, face a daunting challenge or fall ill. Yet that is precisely the time to become even bolder. Those who are victors at heart are the greatest of all champions.

I VIEW THINGS through the Buddha eye,
I see the living beings in the six paths,
how poor and distressed they are, without merit or wisdom,
how they enter the perilous road of birth and death,
their sufferings continuing with never a break,
how deeply they are attached to the five desires,
like a yak enamored of its tail,
blinding themselves with greed and infatuation,
their vision so impaired they can see nothing.
They do not seek the Buddha, with his great might,
or the Law that can end their sufferings,
but enter deeply into erroneous views,
hoping to shed suffering through greater suffering.
For the sake of these living beings
I summon up a mind of great compassion.

—*The Lotus Sutra*

THE AIR around us is filled with radio waves of various frequencies. While these are invisible, a television set can collect them and turn them into visible images. The practice of chanting Nam-myoho-renge-kyo aligns the rhythm of our own lives with the world of Buddhahood in the universe. It "tunes" our lives, so to speak, so that we can manifest the power of Buddhahood in our very beings.

ONE'S ACTIONS in previous existences are all engraved in and contained in this lifetime. The causes for our present suffering or joy, happiness or misery, all lie in our own past actions. But Nichiren Buddhism enables us to fundamentally reform our destiny. When we truly base ourselves on Buddhism's view of life's eternity, we realize the first thing to change is how we live in the present. In Nichiren Buddhism, change arises from the depths of our being. Strong, pure vitality abundantly wells forth. The iron chains of destiny are cut, and our original identity, the fresh and robust world of Buddhahood, appears.

SUCH THINGS as money, fame and material posses-
sions offer a fleeting satisfaction, something that can
be called relative happiness. However, when we transform our lives internally, when we develop within ourselves a brilliant inner palace, then we can be said to
have established absolute happiness. If we develop a
state of mind as vast and resplendent as a magnificent
palace, then nothing—no matter where we go or what
we may encounter in life—can undermine or destroy
our happiness.

OCTOBER
19

OUR INDIVIDUAL experiences of triumph over our problems give courage and hope to many others. Our personal victories, in other words, become parables expressing the power of the Mystic Law. And those who hear our experiences can share them with still others.

WE SHOULD all develop the mind to rejoice in, praise and share in the gift of those who have artistic talents and a richness of heart, whether they achieve wide recognition or not. Cultivating such a beautiful mind is a very worthy effort. Culture and art are not just decorations. They are not just accessories. What matters is whether culture enriches the essential substance of our lives.

OUR LIVES grow to the degree that we give hope and courage to others and enable them to develop their lives. Therefore, while we speak of practicing Buddhism for others, it is we ourselves who ultimately benefit. With this understanding comes the ability to take action with a sense of appreciation.

ANY POSITION, honor or wealth we may gain we will possess only during our present existence. But the unshakable state of life we develop through faith in Nam-myoho-renge-kyo represents our greatest spiritual treasure.

THE MISFORTUNE of others is our misfortune. Our happiness is the happiness of others. To see ourselves in others and feel an inner oneness and sense of unity with them represents a fundamental revolution in the way we view and live our lives. Therefore, discriminating against another person is the same as discriminating against oneself. When we hurt another, we are hurting ourselves. And when we respect others, we respect and elevate our own lives as well.

WHAT ONE has done for another yesterday will be done for oneself today. Blossoms turn into fruit, and brides become mothers-in-law. Chant Nam-myoho-renge-kyo, and be always diligent in your faith.

—*Nichiren*

HEALTH IS NOT simply a matter of absence of illness. Health means constant challenge. Constant creativity. A prolific life always moving forward, opening up fresh new vistas—that is a life of true health. An unbeatable spirit is what supplies the power to keep pressing ahead.

OCTOBER
26

BUDDHISM is a movement emphasizing self-education with the aim of unlocking and developing our inherent Buddha nature while at the same time bringing forth diverse wisdom and using various expedient means to help others tap their Buddhahood. This development of potential, this education of oneself and others, is the noblest path a human being can ever pursue.

L ITERATURE that works to refine, deepen and save the human soul is akin to a religion that elevates and binds people together. And the texts of great religions, such as the Bible and the Buddhist scriptures, make great literature. Literature and religion are parts of the human heritage, and determining how to use that heritage is essential to our further growth as human beings.

SHAKYAMUNI BUDDHA explained the fundamental spirit of Buddhism as a sense of individual responsibility. "You are your only master. Who else? Subdue yourself and discover your master." In other words, we must each take responsibility for our own self-discipline and for cultivating meaningful lives.

A<small>S YOU MEET</small> various trials and difficulties, thus polishing all the many facets of the jewel which is life, you will learn to walk that supreme pathway of humanity. Of this, I am confident, and I am confident too that those who embrace life's native creativity now stand and will continue to stand in the vanguard of history. Bringing the creativity of life to its fullest flowering is the work of human revolution. Carrying out this kind of human revolution is your mission now as it will be throughout your lives.

IF **YOU ALLOW** the passing of time to let you forget the lofty vows of your youth, you stand to block the source of your own boundless good fortune and sever the roots of limitless prosperity for your family and loved ones as well. Please never let this happen. Only by remaining steadfast to the vows we have made in our youth can we shine as true victors in life.

DEATH DOES NOT discriminate; it strips of us everything. Fame, wealth and power are all useless in the unadorned reality of the final moments of life. When the time comes, we will have only ourselves to rely on. This is a solemn confrontation that we must face armed only with our raw humanity, the actual record of what we have done, how we have chosen to live our lives, asking, "Have I lived true to myself? What have I contributed to the world? What are my satisfactions or regrets?"

NOVEMBER

BUDDHISM is not a religion that closes its eyes to people's suffering; it is a teaching that opens people's eyes. Therefore, Buddhism is the path that enables people to become happy. To turn away our eyes from the contradictions of society and rid ourselves of all worldly thoughts is not the way of Buddhist practice.

The true spirit of meditation lies in manifesting our innate wisdom in society and resolutely struggling for the happiness of ourselves and others, and to construct a better society.

THE LOTUS SUTRA explains that the self is one with the universe. The practice of the Lotus Sutra is the practice of compassion to respect and revere everyone as a treasure tower, and to become happy conjointly with others in accord with the principle of the oneness of self and others, while overcoming the various difficulties we face.

THE LOTUS SUTRA is a scripture to be practiced. Its teachings are meant to be put into action. Our faith and study of Buddhist doctrine are enhanced and given life through actual practice. Nichiren Buddhism is not a teaching of quiet contemplation and meditation; it is a teaching of action. Failing to translate the teachings of Buddhism into action is to go against Buddhism's fundamental spirit.

TRUST is difficult to earn and it is easily lost—the trust built over a decade can be shattered in an instant by one offhanded remark or deed. A person who is not swayed from their chosen path, even during the most trying times, will ultimately find that he or she is trusted by all.

EACH OF YOU should summon up the courage of a lion king and never succumb to threats from anyone. The lion king fears no other beast, nor do its cubs. Slanderers are like barking foxes, but Nichiren's followers are like roaring lions.

—Nichiren

NOVEMBER

6

SOCIETY is where we put the teachings of Buddhism into practice. The essence of Buddhism shines in our actions in society.

TRUE EASE and comfort are not found in a quiet, uneventful life. This may sound paradoxical, but hardships bring about ease and comfort. For only by establishing strong individual lives capable of boldly challenging difficult obstacles can we find true "peace and security in this lifetime," as the Lotus Sutra says.

NOVEMBER

8

THE NOTED pacifist scholar Johan Galtung tells young people, "We must be realists in our brains while keeping the flame of idealism burning in our hearts." Both of these—to see the world as it is and how it could be—are essential to reform. A firm hold on reality should not entail being swamped by or resting easy in the status quo. To pioneer uncharted ways requires that people today keep the lamp of optimism lit.

DON'T PUT on airs. Conceit and pretense don't win people's hearts; the façade soon crumbles. Be yourself. Buddhism teaches we can shine most brilliantly through natural, unaffected behavior. Being sincere, dedicated and honest is the key. People of integrity triumph in the end.

OUR LIVES are our own. It is not for someone else to dictate to us how we should live them. All that awaits those who allow themselves to be continually swayed by what other people say or do is unhappiness. We simply need to have the self-belief to be able to say: "This is right. This is the path I will follow. I am content." Happiness is born from such inner fortitude.

A SENSE of being part of the great all-inclusive life prompts us to reflect on our own place and on how we ought to live. Guarding others' lives, the ecology and the earth is the same as protecting one's own life. By like token, wounding them is the same thing as wounding oneself. Consequently, it is the duty of each of us to participate as members of the life community in the evolution of the universe. We can do this by guarding earth's ecological system.

INDULGENCE and indolence produce nothing creative. Complaints and evasions reflect a cowardly spirit; they corrupt and undermine life's natural creative thrust. When life is denuded of the will to struggle creatively, it sinks into a state of hellish destructiveness directed at all that lives.

NICHIREN WRITES, "None of you who declare your-selves to be my disciples should ever give way to cowardice." When the crucial moment comes, it is important to battle through it with the ferocity of a charging lion. This is the key to creating a record of last-ing brilliance. As the ancient Greek poet and playwright Euripides inscribed, "Courage is very powerful against misfortune."

OUR VOICE resonates with life. Because this is so, it can touch the lives of others. The caring and compassion imbued in your voice finds passage to the listener's soul, striking his or her heart and causing it to sing out; the human voice summons something profound from deep within, and can even compel a person into action.

WE ARE ALWAYS changing. If you decide passively, "I'm a quiet type now, so I'll just go through life being quiet," then you won't fully realize your unique potential. On the other hand, you can challenge yourself to become someone, who, though quiet and reserved by nature, will nevertheless say what needs to be said at the right moment, clearly and completely, someone who has the courage to speak out and stand up for the truth.

THE REAL essence and practice of humanism is found in heartfelt, one-to-one dialogue. Be it summit diplomacy or the various interactions of private citizens in different lands, genuine dialogue has the kind of intensity described by the great twentieth-century humanist and philosopher Martin Buber as an encounter "on the narrow ridge" in which the slightest inattention could result in a precipitous fall. Dialogue is indeed this kind of intense, high-risk encounter.

THE LOTUS SUTRA, which explains that all people can attain Buddhahood and that all people are Buddhas, embodies a spirit of supreme respect for human beings. By contrast, those teachings and ideas that seek to turn people into objects to be exploited embody ultimate disrespect for human beings. Such disrespect is an expression of fundamental darkness.

On the level of the individual, practicing the Lotus Sutra means confronting the fundamental darkness in one's own life.

IF YOU WANT to build a happy life, you have to give careful thought to the foundations. Happiness certainly cannot be secured on appearances or affectation. Happiness comes down to the inner state of our life at a given moment.

To BE CONCERNED only with one's own happiness is egoism. To claim you care only about the happiness of others is hypocrisy. Genuine happiness is becoming happy together with others. Josei Toda said: "Just becoming happy oneself—there's nothing difficult to that. It's easy. Helping others become happy is the foundation of our faith."

MANY THINGS happen in life. There are joyous days and times of suffering. Sometimes unpleasant things occur. But that's what makes life so interesting. The dramas we encounter are part and parcel of being human. If we experienced no change or drama in our lives, if nothing unexpected ever happened, we would merely be like automatons, our lives unbearably monotonous and dull. Therefore, please develop a strong self so that you can enact the drama of your life with confidence and poise in the face of whatever vicissitudes you may encounter.

EVERYONE born in this world has a unique role that only he or she can fulfill. Were this not the case, we would not be here. The universe never acts without cause; everything invariably has a reason for being. Even the weeds people love to loathe serve a purpose.

WISDOM, not might, is the most important thing. Wisdom and compassion are deeply connected. Giving earnest thought to others' welfare, asking ourselves what can we do to help—using our minds in this way is a sign of compassion.

THE PURPOSE of Buddhism is to bring out the Buddha nature that all people inherently possess, to awaken people to it and enable them to attain Buddhahood. Moreover, the Lotus Sutra does not allow for any discrimination; all people are equally entitled to salvation.

THERE IS NO ONE lonelier or more unhappy than a person who does not know the pure joy of creating a life for himself or herself. To be human is not merely to stand erect and manifest intelligence or knowledge. To be human in the full sense of the word is to lead a creative life.

The struggle to create new life from within is a truly wonderful thing. There is found the brilliant wisdom that guides and directs the workings of reason; the light of insight that penetrates the farthest reaches of the universe; the undaunted will to see justice done that meets and challenges all the assaults of evil; the spirit of unbounded care that embraces all who suffer. When these are fused with that energy of compassion that pours forth from the deepest sources of cosmic life, an ecstatic rhythm arises to color the lives of all people.

SUPPOSE THAT a person is standing at the foot of a tall embankment and is unable to ascend. And suppose that there is someone on top of the embankment who lowers a rope and says, "If you take hold of this rope, I will pull you up to the top of the embankment." If the person at the bottom begins to doubt that the other has the strength to pull him up, or wonders if the rope is not too weak and therefore refuses to put forth his hand and grasp it, then how is he ever to get to the top of the embankment? But if he follows the instructions, puts out his hand, and takes hold of the rope, then he can climb up.

—*Nichiren*

L IFE IS LONG. The important thing is to remain true to a lofty goal to the very end. Buddhism enables you to adorn the final chapter of your life with brilliant success, just as the golden sun colors the sky in glorious crimson hues and beams of sublime light. To do so, you need to keep making efforts year after year and winning year after year.

THE TRUE VICTORS in life are those who, enduring repeated challenges and setbacks, have sent the roots of their being to such a depth that nothing can shake them.

MANY YOUNG WOMEN agonize over perceived personality flaws and a lack of self-confidence. Nichiren Buddhism, however, teaches the great path of human revolution that enables each of us to shine in our own unique way. With this philosophy, you can decisively overcome a weak and easily swayed life-state and become a person of strength and purpose. It will allow you to withstand the storms of suffering and build a rock-solid foundation that will support you throughout your entire precious lives.

DO NOT become subservient. Do not dwell on every tiny setback in the course of pursuing your chosen path. To do so would be foolish. Victory or defeat is determined by our entire lives. Moreover, our final years are the most crucial.

What is enviable about the pretentious rich? What is great about conceited celebrities? What is admirable about political leaders who gained their positions of power by treating others with contempt? Dig right where you stand, for there lies a rich wellspring!

THAT WE TAKE pains to protect weapons while we expose children—the future of the race—to peril is impermissible. To ignore this absurdity will spell defeat for humanity. We must not live to destroy. We have the spiritual power to create peace and happiness.

DECEMBER

THE MAIN THING is to be proud of the work you do, to live true to yourself. Activity is another name for happiness. What's important is that you give free, unfettered play to your unique talents, that you live with the full radiance of your being. This is what it means to be truly alive.

WHAT IS DEFEAT in life? It is not merely making a mistake; defeat means giving up on yourself in the midst of difficulty. What is true success in life? True success means winning in your battle with yourself. Those who persist in the pursuit of their dreams, no matter what the hurdles, are winners in life, for they have won over their weaknesses.

DIALOGUE is a positive endeavor. It builds solidarity and creates unity. To reject others only has negative repercussions. It invites division and leads to destruction. The point is to meet and to talk. It is only natural that our perspective may at times differ from that of others. But dialogue gives rise to trust, even among those who don't see eye-to-eye.

NICHIREN reminds us: "It is the heart that is important." It is in the heart of faith that Buddhahood resides and boundless and immeasurable happiness shines forth.

Happiness is not something located far away. We must realize that it exists within our own lives. Nichiren Buddhism teaches this and shows us how to attain indestructible happiness.

DECEMBER

5

INCONSPICUOUS virtue brings conspicuous reward. From the perspective of Buddhism, we never fail to receive the effect of our actions, whether good or bad; therefore, it's meaningless to be two-faced or to pretend to be something we're not.

HUMAN SOCIETY can be full of contradictions. It can be unfair, unforgiving, too. Yet we cannot afford to turn our backs to the world. A person who does loses, and no excuse can gloss that over. Given a choice whether to sink or swim, one must swim to the very end, no matter how the seas around us may rage.

PEACE CAN never be attained by passively waiting for it. It is necessary for each of us, no matter how weak we may feel we are, to build deep within our hearts a stronghold for peace that can withstand, and in the end silence, the incessant calls for war.

EDUCATION allows us to be truly human. It deepens us and enables us to build a better society and a brighter future. The profundity of education determines the profundity of culture, the nature of society and the firmness of peace. Education plays a major role in creating deep solidarity, mutual understanding and trust.

FLORENCE NIGHTINGALE, the founder of the modern nursing profession, proudly declared: "Let us be anxious to do well, not for selfish praise but to honor and advance the cause, the work we have taken up." The spirit to fulfill a noble mission is pure, strong, and beautiful. It is a spirit that we all should emulate.

RALPH WALDO EMERSON once wrote: "Women are, by their power of conversation and their social influence, the civilizers of mankind. What is civilization? I answer, the power of good women." The solidarity of wise, good women will be the great power to guide the world toward peace and happiness.

WHEN A TREE has been transplanted, though fierce winds may blow, it will not topple if it has a firm stake to hold it up. But even a tree that has grown up in place may fall over if its roots are weak. Even a feeble person will not stumble if those supporting him are strong, but a person of considerable strength, when alone, may fall down on an uneven path.

—*Nichiren*

HAPPINESS IS a matter of the heart. This is not mere spiritualism. Our hearts are precious vessels endowed with the treasure of Buddhahood. When we strive earnestly in faith and practice and reveal our Buddhahood, we can walk along the sure and steady path to happiness and attain a state of complete fulfillment and satisfaction. Nichiren writes: "Fortune comes from one's heart and makes one worthy of respect."

LIFE IS a chain. All things are related. When any link is disturbed, the other links will be affected. We should think of the environment as our mother—Mother Soil, Mother Sea, Mother Earth. There is no crime worse than harming one's mother.

YOUR HAPPINESS and victory in life hinge on whether you can grasp, while you are still young, the fact that happiness lies within. That's why there is no need for you to compare yourselves to others but instead strive powerfully and cheerfully to develop your state of life, aiming to improve yourselves each day. From that struggle will bloom noble flowers of mission, flowers of happiness that are yours and yours alone. Shine as you are, live true to yourselves and advance in your own unique way.

To challenge yourselves to your heart's content in your youth so that you are left with no regrets later, to grow, to make dynamic strides forward—this is the noblest way to live. Victory in youth leads to victory in life.

A SOCIETY that has sacrificed so much to material wealth that it has forgotten the human heart and the better human aspirations degenerates into something compassionless, doctrinaire, ignorant and ultraconservative. When this happens, fundamental solutions to calamities become impossible. If we protect the truth and are resolute, we are capable of creating peace and prosperity. And the truth we must protect ought to be high and great.

Our great truth—the thing that we must protect to the utmost—involves ethics and the best of human nature. But more basic than anything else is our duty to guard the truth of life, the truth that we and the universe are one, and that a single ordinary human thought contains the entirety of universal life.

THERE IS NO self-improvement without effort. Without taking action, happiness will never come, no matter how long you wait. A life without peaks and valleys is a fairy tale. Reality is strict, because it is a win-or-lose struggle. This is the way it is for human beings. Therefore, you should not allow yourselves to be battered about by reality but rather willingly rise to its challenges and use them as opportunities to train and strengthen yourselves.

18

L IVE WITH a dancing spirit. The stars in the heavens are dancing through space, the earth never ceases to spin. All life is dancing: the trees with the wind, the waves on the sea, the birds, the fish, all are performing their own dance of life. Every living thing is dancing, and you must keep dancing too, for the rest of your life!

DECEMBER
19

RELATIONSHIP problems are opportunities to grow and mature. Such problems can be character building if you don't let them defeat you. That's why it's important not to isolate yourself. No one can exist apart from others. Remaining aloof from others cultivates self-ishness, which accomplishes nothing.

CREATION IS quite different from mere ideas. Even ideas require fundamental and extensive speculative accumulation. It goes without saying that creation in learning demands an incomparably greater fundamental ability. The task of creation is like a lofty mountain whose summit is formed only when there exist vast slopes and a solid foundation. Likewise, the fruitful work of creation can only be attained when it is based on the extensive knowledge of learning and profound speculation.

EVEN IF TODAY may seem to be a time of total darkness, it will not last forever. The dawn will surely come if you advance, ever forward, without being defeated. The day will definitely come when you can look back fondly and declare, "I am savoring this happiness because I struggled back then." It is those who know the bitterness of winter that can savor the true joy of spring.

EVEN IF you are born into the most affluent of circumstances or enjoy a spectacular marriage that is the envy of others, there is no guarantee that you will be happy. Happiness does not depend on wealth or personal appearance, nor does it hinge on fame or recognition. If your heart is empty, you cannot build genuine happiness.

There is an expansive life-state of profound, secure happiness that transcends any material or social advantage. It is called faith; it is called the life-state of Buddhahood.

PEACE and culture are one. A genuinely cultured nation is a peaceful nation, and vice versa. When conflicts multiply, culture wanes and nations fall into a hellish existence. The history of the human race is a contrast between culture and barbarity. Only culture is a force strong enough to put an end to conflict and lead humanity in the direction of peace.

WHERE IS HAPPINESS to be found? The famous Roman philosopher-emperor Marcus Aurelius said, "A man's true delight is to do the things he was made for." Human happiness, he maintained, lies in doing those things only humans can: seeking the truth and acting to help those who are suffering. Johann Wolfgang von Goethe, too, asserted that those who work cheerfully and take joy in the fruits of their labor are truly happy. These are the words of great thinkers, and as you can see they are in complete accord with the teachings of Buddhism.

BUDDHISM does not ask "What religion does this person follow?" but "What is this person's state of life?" Buddhism exists to enable all people to cultivate and manifest the world of Buddhahood in their lives. Society is a realm of discrimination and distinctions. But Buddhism transcends all superficial differences and focuses directly on life.

IT IS FOOLISH to ignore or deny the contribution of medicine. Otherwise, faith descends into fanaticism. We must use medical resources wisely in fighting illness. Buddhism gives us the wisdom to use medicine properly. Wisdom is the basic ingredient to health, to long life and to happiness. The new century of health, then, must be a new century of wisdom.

RELIGIOUS STRIFE must be avoided at all cost; under no circumstance should it be allowed. People may hold different religious beliefs, but the bottom line is that we are all human beings. We all seek happiness and desire peace. Religion should bring people together. It should unite the potential for good in people's hearts toward benefiting society and humanity and creating a better future.

THOSE WHO believe in the Lotus Sutra are as if in winter, but winter always turns to spring. Never, from ancient times on, has anyone heard or seen of winter turning back to autumn. Nor have we ever heard of a believer in the Lotus Sutra who turned into an ordinary person. The sutra reads, "If there are those who hear the Law, then not a one will fail to attain Buddhahood."

—*Nichiren*

RALPH WALDO EMERSON writes, "And so of cheerfulness, or a good temper, the more it is spent, the more of it remains." Cheerfulness is not the same as frivolousness. Cheerfulness is born of a fighting spirit. Frivolousness is the reverse side of cowardly escape. Emerson also said that "power dwells with cheerfulness; hope puts us in a working mood." Without cheerfulness there is no strength. Strive to advance still more brightly and cheerfully.

D EFEAT for a Buddhist lies not in encountering difficulties but rather in not challenging them. Difficulties only truly become our destiny if we run away from
them. We must fight as long as we live.

BUDDHISM ENABLES us to tap from within the depths of our beings the greatest courage and strongest life force there is. Buddhas are not destined for unhappiness or defeat. Those who practice Buddhism can definitely transform all adversity into something positive, irrespective of the troubled time in which they live, their personal circumstances or the hardships that befall them.

INDEX

greater self, 171, 219. *See also* Buddha nature; lesser self

growth, achieving individual and organization, 32; power of, 66; process to, 139

happiness, 208, 393; achieving, 51; another name for, 377; attaining true, 287; Marcus Aurelius on, 400; common view of, 398; condition to savor, 222; creating our, 73, 354, 374; finding, 96, 126, 380, 390; formula for, 24; genuine, 224, 363; path to, 49, 281, 388; securing, 362; seed of, 181; sense of, 280; throughout eternity, 127; Josei Toda on, 363; two kinds of, 241

hardships, a Buddha and, 298; transforming, 185; viewing, with Nichiren Buddhism, 118; welcoming, 351

hatred, overcoming, 36

health, Buddhism and, 70; life of true, 335

heart, positive and negative functions of the, 53; power of the human, 254

hell, Nichiren on, 48; life-state of, 356

"Hero of the World," the Buddha's title, 17

Hesse, Herman, 286

history, creating individual, 318

home, Buddhist view of the, 306; building a happy, 154

hope, power of, 66

Hugo, Victor, 137

human, becoming, 166; being, 368

human beings, becoming exemplary, 353; cause of becoming shallow, 102; developing identity as, 157; "enjoy themselves at ease" and, 40; noblest path of, 336; reason to be born, 40; and spiritual strength and, 227; Josei Toda and, 40; yardstick to measure merit as, 196

human revolution, 103, 180, 192, 214, 231, 261, 328; path of, 372; process of, 119; realizing our personal, 250; work of, 339

human rights, 39

human spirit, 31

humanity, Buddhist view of, 290; cultivating our, 109; developing true, 131, 237; genuine, 67; practice of revealing, 360; true, 67, 292

humankind, changing destiny of, 69, 214; transforming destiny of, 155

hypocrisy, 363

ideals, dedication to noble, 156; foundation to alight, 80

identity, establishing a sense of, 262; uncovering your true, 58

illness, Buddhist view of, 300

illusions, source of, 121

incompetence, cause of intellectual, 269

individuality, refined, 71; taking pride in, 152; true, 63

individuals, becoming outstanding, 82

institutions, individual transforming large, 158

integrity, having, 353

interaction, human, 42

isolation, cultivates selfishness, 395

jealousy, 237

joy, cause of present, 327; deriving true, 179; savoring true, 397

Jung, Carl, 171

justice, people of, 267; Josei Toda on, 235

karma, concept of, 217; Nichiren Buddhism and, 285

mastering mind, 41; on overcoming sufferings of birth and death, 18; spirit of,
292; on strong faith, 247; on suffering and
joy, 151; on treasuring life, 206
Nightingale, Florence, 385

objectives, achieving great, 226
obstacles, attitude when encountering, 149
old age, outlook on, 92
oneness of life and environment, 261
optimism, Buddhist, 249; maintaining, 194;
true, 68
ordinary being, 207, 288; Nichiren on, 13,
140, 293

parents, and children, 75; mission of, 174
peace, 289; accomplishing, 35; actualizing
and guarding, 61; creating, 374, 392;
and culture, 399; establishing, within
ourselves, 383; path to, 399;
winning, 21
"peace and security in this lifetime," finding
true, 351
people, deficit of good-natured, 267; winning heart of, 353
peril, cause of, 61
perseverance, 181, 189, 315
person, forward-looking, 260; scale to
measure worth of, 265
perspective, shallow, 197
phenomena, life and, 95
philosophy, purpose of, 262
pioneer, becoming a, 352
poetic spirit, power of possessing a, 175
politician, role of a, 279
potential, actualizing, 359
practices, peaceful, 283

prayers, 30, 181; continual, 97; correct way
of, 282; Nichiren on, 273; in Nichiren
Buddhism, 250; path to actualize, 124;
power of, 203; struggles and, 102. *See also*
vow
prejudice, Nichiren on, 301
pretense, 353
problems. *See* sufferings
promptness, 114
prosperity, cause of, 392

reading, benefits of, 109
realists, 23
reality, confronting, 393
"realizing your inherent potential," concept
of, 71
reason, religion and, 122
The Record of the Orally Transmitted Teachings, 283
regret, life without, 204
relationships, confrontations in, 215; dealing
with unhappy, 160; nagging, 215; surmounting painful, 34; viewing problems
of, 395
relative happiness, 328
religions, avoiding conflicts among, 403;
guideline of, in twenty-first century, 252;
origin of, 240; purpose of, 116, 262;
rationality and, 43; standard to evaluate
validity of, 205
resolutions, honoring, 182
resolve, inner, 56, 158
respect, 184, 333; characterizing lives worthy of, 284; path to mutual, 195
responsibility, 81
restrictions, advancing within set of, 199
reverence for life, practicing ideal of, 128
reward, inconspicuous, 381